LEITCH
Review of Skills

Prosperity for all in the global economy
- world class skills

Final Report

December 2006

£18.00

Contacts

This document can be found on the Leitch Review of Skills website at:

hm-treasury.gov.uk/leitch

For general enquiries about HM Treasury and its work, contact:

Correspondence and Enquiry Unit
HM Treasury
1 Horse Guards Road
London
SW1A 2HQ

Tel: 020 7270 4558
Fax: 020 7270 4861
E-mail: public.enquiries@hm-treasury.gov.uk

ISBN-10: 0-11-840486-5
ISBN-13: 978-0-11-840486-0

Printed by The Stationery Office   12/06   349624

PU061

Contents

FOREWORD

In the 19th Century, the UK had the natural resources, the labour force and the inspiration to lead the world into the Industrial Revolution. Today, we are witnessing a different type of revolution. For developed countries who cannot compete on natural resources and low labour costs, success demands a more service-led economy and high value-added industry.

In the 21st Century, our natural resource is our people – and their potential is both untapped and vast. Skills will unlock that potential. The prize for our country will be enormous – higher productivity, the creation of wealth and social justice.

The alternative? Without increased skills, we would condemn ourselves to a lingering decline in competitiveness, diminishing economic growth and a bleaker future for all.

The case for action is compelling and urgent. Becoming a world leader in skills will enable the UK to compete with the best in the world. I am very optimistic.

I was asked by the Government in 2004 to consider what the UK's long-term ambition should be for developing skills in order to maximise economic prosperity, productivity and to improve social justice.

This challenge is formidable. Skills matter fundamentally for the economic and social health of the UK. I have listened to key stakeholders and eminent thinkers at home and abroad. There is consensus that we need to be much more ambitious and a clear message that the UK must 'raise its game'.

Today the UK is in a strong position with a stable and growing economy. We have world-leading employment rates. However, we cannot be complacent and we cannot predict future economic conditions with certainty, but we do know that demand for skills will grow inexorably.

Demographic, technological and global changes present enormous challenges and brilliant opportunities. The population continues to age. Technological developments are occurring faster than we dreamed, dramatically altering the way we work. Competitive pressures on all sectors of the economy are increasing. Manufactured goods, and increasingly services, are traded across the world. Developed nations are relying more and more on their capacity to innovate to drive economic growth. The ability to do this depends upon the skills and knowledge of their people.

Our nation's skills are not world class and we run the risk that this will undermine the UK's long-term prosperity. Productivity continues to trail many of our main international comparators. Despite recent progress, the UK has serious social disparities with high levels of child poverty, poor employment rates for the disadvantaged, regional disparities and relatively high income inequality. Improving our skill levels can address all of these problems.

How is the UK placed to respond to this challenge? We have many important strengths – an excellent higher education system where more people then ever are studying for degrees; many good initiatives on vocational training; an increasingly effective school system; and a strong record of improvement over the past decade.

We also have very considerable weaknesses. Today, more than one third of adults do not hold the equivalent of a basic school-leaving qualification. Almost one half of adults (17 million) have difficulty with numbers and one seventh (5 million) are not functionally literate. This is worse than our principal comparators. Continuing to improve our schools will not be enough to solve these problems. Today, over 70 per cent of our 2020 workforce have already completed their compulsory education.

Our intermediate and technical skills lag countries such as Germany and France. We have neither the quantity nor the quality of necessary vocational skills. We have made enormous progress expanding higher education – and this is critical to becoming a high-skill economy. Over one quarter of adults hold a degree, but this is less than many of our key comparators, who also invest more. Our skills base compares poorly and, critically, all of our comparators are improving. Being world class is a moving target.

It is clear from my analysis that, despite substantial investment and reform plans already in place, by 2020, we will have managed only to 'run to stand still'. On our current trajectory, the UK's comparative position will not have improved significantly. In the meantime, the world will have continued to change and the global environment will be even harsher. The scale of the challenge is daunting.

Our recommendations start with an ambitious vision. The UK must become a world leader in skills. Skills is the most important lever within our control to create wealth and to reduce social deprivation.

We recommend radical change right across the skills spectrum. We have defined clear ambitions at basic, intermediate and higher skills. Our study focuses on adult skills but we express concern and suggest action for 14-19s.

'Economically valuable skills' is our mantra. Institutional change and simplification are necessary. However, we have tried to identify how to deliver better on what we have rather than to invent many more new structures.

Too many of us have little interest or appetite for improved skills. We must begin a new journey to embed a culture of learning. Employer and individual awareness must increase.

To reach our goals, we as a society must invest more. It is clear who will pay. It is all of us – it is the State, employers and individuals. But this will be the best investment we could ever make.

We have worked closely with the Devolved Administrations in Northern Ireland, Scotland and Wales. While many of our recommendations are specific to England, the issues are common to the four countries. The Devolved Administrations are analysing what best applies to them.

We look forward to a considered response.

This has been a complicated task and hard work. I acknowledge the support, advice and encouragement from many people. Thank you.

Sandy Leitch

Lord Leitch

EXECUTIVE SUMMARY

The Leitch Review was tasked in 2004 with considering the UK's long-term skills needs. The UK is building on economic strength and stability, with 14 years of unbroken growth and the highest employment rate in the G7. Its skills base has improved significantly over the last decade with rising school standards and growth in graduate numbers. Despite this, the UK's skills base remains weak by international standards, holding back productivity, growth and social justice. The Review has found that, even if current targets to improve skills are met, the UK's skills base will still lag behind that of many comparator countries in 2020. The UK will run to stand still.

The global economy is changing rapidly, with emerging economies such as India and China growing dramatically, altering UK competitiveness. The population is ageing, technological change and global migration flows are increasing. There is a direct correlation between skills, productivity and employment. Unless the UK can build on reforms to schools, colleges and universities and make its skills base one of its strengths, UK businesses will find it increasingly difficult to compete. As a result of low skills, the UK risks increasing inequality, deprivation and child poverty, and risks a generation cut off permanently from labour market opportunity. The best form of welfare is to ensure that people can adapt to change. Skills were once *a* key lever for prosperity and fairness. Skills are now increasingly *the* key lever. A radical step-change is necessary.

A compelling vision for the UK. The Review recommends that the UK commit to becoming a world leader in skills by 2020, benchmarked against the upper quartile of the OECD. This means doubling attainment at most levels. Stretching objectives for 2020 include*:

- 95 per cent of adults to achieve the basic skills of functional literacy and numeracy, an increase from levels of 85 per cent literacy and 79 per cent numeracy in 2005;

- exceeding 90 per cent of adults qualified to at least Level 2, an increase from 69 per cent in 2005. A commitment to go further and achieve 95 per cent as soon as possible;

- shifting the balance of intermediate skills from Level 2 to Level 3. Improving the esteem, quantity and quality of intermediate skills. This means 1.9 million additional Level 3 attainments over the period and boosting the number of Apprentices to 500,000 a year;

- exceeding 40 per cent of adults qualified to Level 4 and above, up from 29 per cent in 2005, with a commitment to continue progression.

Principles. The following principles underpin delivery of a raised ambition:

- shared responsibility. Employers, individuals and the Government must increase action and investment. Employers and individuals should contribute most where they derive the greatest private returns. Government investment must focus on market failures, ensuring a basic platform of skills for all, targeting help where it is needed most;

- focus on economically valuable skills. Skill developments must provide real returns for individuals, employers and society. Wherever possible, skills should be portable to deliver mobility in the labour market for individuals and employers;

---

* Broad definitions. Adults means age 19 to State Pension age. Basic means everyday literacy and numeracy skills. Level 2 equates to 5 good GCSEs; Level 3 equates to 2 'A' levels; Level 4 equates to a degree (or their vocational equivalents).

- **demand-led skills.** The skills system must meet the needs of individuals and employers. Vocational skills must be demand-led rather than centrally planned;

- **adapt and respond.** No one can accurately predict future demand for particular skill types. The framework must adapt and respond to future market needs; and

- **build on existing structures.** Don't always chop and change. Instead, improve performance of current structures through simplification and rationalisation, stronger performance management and clearer remits. Continuity is important.

The Prize for the UK. The prize for achieving this ambition is great – a more prosperous and fairer society. The Review estimates a possible net benefit of at least £80 billion over 30 years. This would come from a boost in the productivity growth rate of up to 15 per cent and an increase in the employment growth rate by around 10 per cent. Social deprivation, poverty and inequality will diminish.

Remit. The Review's remit is to focus on adult skills. This is because 70 per cent of the 2020 working age population have already left compulsory education and the flow of young people will reduce. However, the Review also recognises how vital effective education for young people is to the new ambition. School standards have improved over the past decade, with more young people than ever achieving five good GCSEs. And yet, more than one in six young people leave school unable to read, write and add up properly. The proportion of young people staying in education past 16 is below OECD average. The Review emphasises how critical reforms to GCSEs are to improve functional literacy and numeracy. The new 14-19 Diplomas must succeed. Once the Government is on track to successfully deliver Diplomas, demonstrated by rising participation at age 17, it should implement a change in the law, so that all young people must remain in full or part-time education or workplace training up to the age of 18.

Main recommendations

- **increase adult skills across all levels.** Progress towards world class is best measured by the number of people increasing skills attainment. The raised ambitions will require additional investment by the State, employers and individuals. The Government is committed to increasing the share of GDP for education and skills. Additional annual investment in skills up to Level 3 will need to rise to £1.5-2 billion by 2020. Increased investment is required in higher education, but costings are difficult to project accurately;

- **route all public funding for adult vocational skills in England**, apart from community learning, through Train to Gain and Learner Accounts by 2010.

- **strengthen employer voice.** Rationalise existing bodies, strengthen the collective voice and better articulate employer views on skills by creating a new Commission for Employment and Skills, reporting to central Government and the devolved administrations. The Commission will manage employer influence on skills, within a national framework of individual rights and responsibilities;

- **increase employer engagement and investment in skills.** Reform, relicense and empower Sector Skills Councils (SSC). Deliver more economically valuable skills by only allowing public funding for vocational qualifications where the content has been approved by SSCs. Expand skills brokerage services for both small and large employers;

- **launch a new 'Pledge' for employers to voluntarily commit to train all eligible employees up to Level 2 in the workplace.** In 2010, review progress of employer delivery. If the improvement rate is insufficient, introduce a statutory entitlement to workplace training at Level 2 in consultation with employers and unions;

- increase employer investment in Level 3 and 4 qualifications in the workplace. **Extend Train to Gain to higher levels. Dramatically increase Apprenticeship volumes. Improve engagement between employers and universities. Increase co-funded workplace degrees. Increase focus on Level 5 and above skills;**
- increase people's aspirations and awareness of the value of skills to them and their families. **Create high profile, sustained awareness programmes. Rationalise existing fragmented 'information silos' and develop a new universal adult careers service; and**
- create a new integrated employment and skills service, **based upon existing structures, to increase sustainable employment and progression. Launch a new programme to improve basic skills for those out of work, embedding this support for disadvantaged people and repeat claimants. Develop a network of employer-led Employment and Skills Boards, building on current models, to influence delivery.**

Impact. These recommendations will have a strong and enduring impact across all sectors of society. For example:

- all individuals will have a greater awareness of the value of skills development and easier access to the opportunities available;
- workless people will have a better chance to find a job through effective diagnosis of their skills needs and greater support as they make the transition into sustainable work;
- low-skilled workers will have more chances to gain a full Level 2 qualification and basic skills in the workplace through Train to Gain, and more control over flexible, rewarding learning through their Learner Account;
- skilled workers will have more opportunities to develop their careers in the workplace, through Apprenticeships, degrees and management and leadership programmes;
- small firms will have easier access to relevant training for their employees. Management skills, competitiveness and productivity will improve;
- employers will have more influence over skills strategy within a simplified system, greater incentives to invest in skills across all levels; advice through expanded skills brokerage and increased assistance for workplace training; and
- skills deficiencies will reduce. Upskilling and portable, economically valuable qualifications throughout the entire workforce will ensure improved labour supply.

The UK will be able to compete with the best in the world. Productivity and employment rates will increase. Poverty and inequality will decrease.

Next steps. This policy framework will deliver world class skills. The UK Government and Devolved Administrations in Northern Ireland, Scotland and Wales must now act to decide detailed next steps. The Government will need to consider value for money, capacity of the system to absorb investment, the balance between private and public investment and the trade off with other priorities when making its investment decisions.

1   The Chancellor of the Exchequer and the Secretary of State for Education and Skills commissioned the Leitch Review in 2004 to examine the UK's optimal skills mix in order to maximise economic growth, productivity and social justice. In addition, the Review was asked by the Chancellor in Budget 2006 to consider how best to integrate employment and skills services.

2   Skills policy in the UK is devolved. The Review has worked closely with the Devolved Administrations in Scotland, Wales and Northern Ireland. Its analysis of the UK's skills needs has implications for the policies and targets of the Devolved Administrations (DAs).

THE CENTRAL IMPORTANCE OF SKILLS

Box 1: What do we mean by skills?

Skills are capabilities and expertise in a particular occupation or activity. There are a large number of different types of skills and they can be split into a number of different categories. Basic skills, such as literacy and numeracy, and generic skills, such as team working and communication, are applicable in most jobs. Specific skills tend to be less transferable between occupations. Most occupations use a mix of different types of skills.

The most common measures of skills are qualifications. On the job training in the workplace is a vital source of skills development and career progression. The Review recognises the importance of looking at these wider definitions of skills. For individuals, they provide portability in the labour market, allowing them to demonstrate the skills they have aquired. For employers, they provide valuable signals when recruiting new workers and also motivate employees to complete their training. Qualifications form a major part of employer recruitment strategies, especially screening candidates prior to interview. As a result, the majority of individuals prefer studying towards a qualification[a] and over one half of employers say they would like to support their employees to gain qualifications through staff training.[b]

Qualifications can be grouped into five different levels: full level 2 equates to 5 good GCSEs or their vocational equivalents, full level 3 to two or more A Levels and level 4 and above to degree level qualifications. Levels of literacy and numeracy tend to be based on surveys or on the proportion of the workforce with English or Maths qualifications.

[a] *National Audit Learning Survey*, 2002.
[b] *The market for qualifications in the UK*, PWC, 2005.

The UK economy   3   The UK is in a strong economic position. Economic growth is unbroken for 14 years, the longest period of economic expansion on record. The UK's employment rate is one of the highest in the G7, with 2 million more people employed now than in 1997. The challenge for the UK is to build on this, further increasing prosperity in a changing and more competitive global economy.

4   The UK economy has changed significantly over time. Today the service sector accounts for around three quarters of the UK economy. Almost 29 million people are employed in the UK. Of these, 3 million are self-employed. Small firms with less than 50 employees, excluding the self-employed, account for around one quarter of employment, with large firms accounting for just under one half. The public sector contains more than 20 per cent of total employment. Improving the UK's economic prosperity will mean responding to the challenges that the different types of employer in the UK face.

Global economic changes

5   The UK's challenge is to drive greater increases in prosperity as the global economy changes fundamentally. Emerging economies, such as India and China, are growing dramatically. In 2005, economic growth in China exceeded 10 per cent. By 2015, China is likely to have become the third largest economy in the world.[1] Technology is rapidly breaking down the barriers between what can and cannot be traded. All work that can be 'digitised', automated, and outsourced can increasingly be done by the most effective and competitive individuals or enterprises, wherever they are located.[2]

6   Greater economic integration has been accompanied by increased global migration flows. Net migration to the UK was 185,000 in 2005.[3] The latest estimates show that around 510,000 people from the A8 accession countries[4] have registered to work in the UK since May 2004. Migration generally has a positive effect, helping to mitigate skills shortages and fill jobs that cannot be filled domestically. However, the perception is that individual competition for jobs increases in the short-term.

7   The Review has found that such changes are rapidly increasing the importance of skills. The Organisation for Economic Co-operation and Development (OECD) stresses that, as emerging economies start to deliver high skills at moderate cost, the OECD countries must themselves reform their skills policy.[5] As the global economy changes, an economy's prosperity will be driven increasingly by its skills base.

Productivity

8   The UK's productivity – how much workers produce – has improved in recent years. Despite this, productivity in the UK still lags behind that of comparator nations: the average French worker produces 20 per cent more per hour than the average UK worker, the average German worker 13 per cent more and the average US worker 18 per cent more. Skills are a key lever within our control to improve productivity in the workplace – one fifth or more of the UK's productivity gap with countries such as France and Germany results from the UK's relatively poor skills. Differences in management practices between the USA and the UK, for example, explain 10 to 15 per cent of the productivity gap in manufacturing between the two countries.[6] This indicates that both skills provision and management are important elements in increasing productivity.

---

[1] Based on market exchange rates. See *Long-term global economic challenges and opportunities for the UK*, HM Treasury, 2004.

[2] Friedman, 2005.

[3] ONS, 2006.

[4] A8 countries are Czech Republic, Estonia, Hungary, Latvia, Lithuania, Poland, Slovakia and Slovenia.

[5] *Education at A Glance*, OECD 2006.

[6] *Management practices across firms and nations*, Bloom et al., LSE-Mckinsey, June 2005.

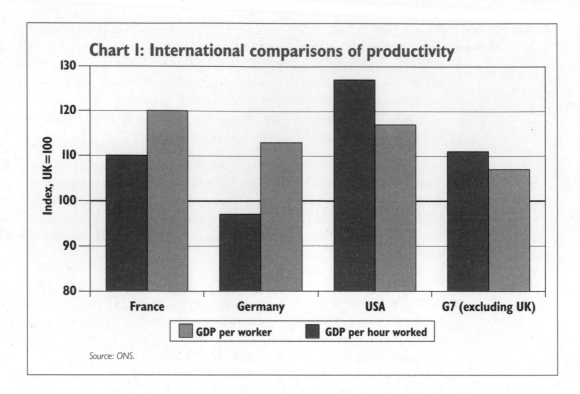

Chart I: International comparisons of productivity

Index, UK=100

GDP per worker | GDP per hour worked

France | Germany | USA | G7 (excluding UK)

Source: ONS.

9   Productivity is increasingly driven by skills. The ability of firms to succeed in the face of growing international competition depends increasingly on the skilled labour force they can draw from. Skilled workers are better able to adapt to new technologies and market opportunities. Higher levels of skills drive innovation, facilitate investment and improve leadership and management. For innovation to be effectively implemented, businesses must be able to draw on a flexible, skilled workforce.

Employment

10   The UK's employment rate – the proportion of the population in work – is one of the highest in the G7 at almost 75 per cent. The employment rate of disadvantaged groups, such as lone parents and people with health problems and disabilities, has risen faster than the average over the past decade. Despite this, more than 20 per cent are economically inactive (not in work or looking for work). Many people in this group want to work. The UK's economy can drive forward even further by increasing the available workforce.

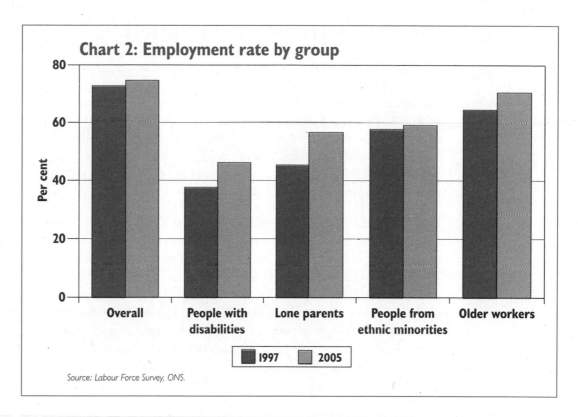

Chart 2: Employment rate by group

Source: Labour Force Survey, ONS.

11   Increasingly, skills are a key determinant of employment – less than one half of those with no qualifications are in work, compared to nearly 90 per cent of those with graduate level qualifications. The employment rate of those with no qualifications has fallen over the past 10 years at a time when the employment rates of most disadvantaged groups have risen more quickly than the average. Lack of skills can be a key barrier to employment for people from some ethnic minorities and other disadvantaged groups.

12   In the new global economy, people's economic security will not depend on trying to protect particular jobs, holding back the tide of change. It is not enough to rely on the traditional model of protecting people from change. Instead, the best form of welfare will be to ensure people can find their next job, staying in the labour market. The best way to do this is to ensure that people have a basic platform of skills that allows flexibility and can update their skills as the economy changes. For people to progress in the modern labour market, they must be able to update their skills to adapt to change. Updating skills and retraining will increase in importance as many of us have longer working lives. World class skills are inexorably tied to world class employment.

Wider benefits 13   Skills are a key driver of fairness; unequal access to skills has contributed to relatively high rates of child poverty and income inequality in the UK. There are clear links between skills and wider social outcomes, such as health, crime and social cohesion. Skills have important impacts on financial capability, helping households to manage the family finances and family life, enabling parents to help their children with their homework.[7]

Critical importance of world class skills 14   To achieve world class prosperity and fairness in the new global economy, the UK must achieve world class skills. Without world class skills, UK businesses will find it increasingly difficult to compete and innovate. The employment opportunities of the lowest skilled will continue to decline, risking a lost generation, cut off permanently from labour market opportunity. The Review has concluded that, where skills were once *a* key driver of prosperity and fairness, they are now *the* key driver. Achieving world class skills is *the* key to achieving economic success and social justice in the new global economy.

---

[7] *Education and skills: The economic benefit*, DfES, 2003.

THE UK'S HISTORIC SKILLS DEFICIT

15   The UK's skills base has suffered from historic deficits built up over a long period of time, despite pockets of excellence. The UK's skills base has improved significantly over recent years as reforms have begun to succeed in driving improvements. The proportion of people with a Level 4 and above qualification has risen from 21 per cent in 1994 to 29 per cent in 2005. The proportion of people with no qualifications has fallen from 22 per cent in 1994 to 13 per cent in 2005. The number of Apprentices in England has grown from 76,000 in 1997 to 256,000 in 2005.[8] Today around 42 per cent of young people age 18-30 participate in higher education, more than ever before.

16   Other countries have also been improving their skills, often from a higher base. As a consequence, the UK's skills base remains mediocre by international standards. In OECD comparisons of 30 countries, the UK lies 17th on low skills, 20th on intermediate and 11th on high skills. 7 million adults lack functional numeracy and 5 million lack functional literacy. 17 million adults lack Level 1 numeracy – equivalent to a low level GCSE. The proportion of people with low or no qualifications is more than double that in Sweden, Japan and Canada. More than 50 per cent of people in countries such as Germany and New Zealand are qualified to intermediate level, compared to fewer than 40 per cent in the UK. The proportion of people with high skills is internationally average, but not world leading. The UK invests 1.1 per cent of GDP in higher education compared to 2.9 per cent in the USA and 2.6 per cent in South Korea.

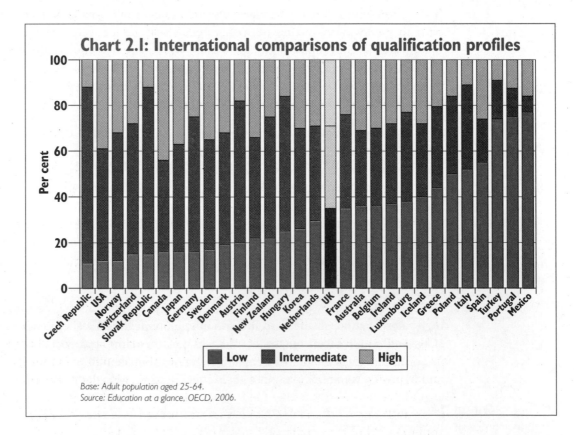

Chart 2.1: International comparisons of qualification profiles

Base: Adult population aged 25-64.
Source: Education at a glance, OECD, 2006.

17   The Review's interim report, published in December 2005, found that the UK's skills base lags behind that of many advanced countries, the product of historic failures in the education and training system. The challenge of delivering economically valuable skills has

---

[8] *Departmental Report*, DfES, 2006.

been a longstanding concern for the UK. Even back in 1776, Adam Smith's *'The Wealth of Nations'* suggested that *'the greater part of what is taught in schools and universities ... does not seem to be the proper preparation for that of business'*.

18   The balance of responsibilities for improving adult skills between government, employers and individuals has changed over time. In 1964, a period of compulsory training activity for employers began with the introduction of Industrial Training Boards (ITBs) and a training levy system. In 1973, the Manpower Services Commission (MSC) was established to plan workforce skill needs, also with statutory powers to improve skills and training among employers. By the 1980s, most of the ITBs were abolished and more voluntarist initiatives and organisations introduced to replace them. These included Training and Enterprise Councils (TECs) in 1989, and National Training Organisations (NTOs) in 1992, as employer-led bodies to assess sectoral and local training needs.

19   The previous system was focused on asking employers to collectively articulate their future skills needs and then trying to plan to meet these needs. Too often, collective articulation of future skills needs has been an ineffective and inefficient mechanism. As a result, too much provision has been supply driven, based on trying to predict and provide. Consequently, employers were reluctant to contribute toward training costs because they did not have confidence in the quality of training on offer and felt frustrated by the lack of influence over qualifications. At the same time, they felt let down by poor levels of basic literacy and numeracy resulting from a failing school system.

20   People were unable to access quality training at a time and place that fitted in with their job, had little choice over training and faced a complex system of financial support. The Government saw its role as protecting people from change through income support, rather than preparing them for it through skills support. It focused on overseeing a training system that tried to predict and provide future skill needs from the centre, rather than empowering people and employers to make the right training decisions for themselves.

21   The impact of this was seen in:

- too little investment by employers in their employees;

- too little responsibility taken by individuals for their own learning;

- a qualification system divorced from the needs of the modern workplace; and

- a welfare system not meeting the needs of people in a fast-changing economy.

Skills in the UK today

22   Over the last decade, the division of responsibilities between government, employers and individuals has continued to evolve. A major recent innovation has been the introduction of the Train to Gain service offering employers workplace training to meet their needs, with public subsidy for training for first, full Level 2 qualifications and support for wider training beyond that level. This 'demand-led' approach is a success. The Employer Training Pilots, on which the rollout of Train to Gain is based, proved effective at engaging employers and employees and are popular with business: 30,000 employers and 250,000 employees had participated by March 2006.[9]

---

[9] ETP Management Information.

23   Currently, employers collectively articulate their qualification needs through their Sector Skills Council (SSC). Their main tasks have been to drive up employer demand for skills and influence provision through drawing up Sector Skills Agreements (SSAs) to ensure that planned provision meets employer needs. They have also had a lead role in developing Sector Qualification Strategies, alongside the Qualifications and Curriculum Authority (QCA) and developing Skills Academies, together with the LSC. There are encouraging signs that the current system of SSCs is bedding down well, with some examples of excellence. However, overall performance is patchy due to conflicting objectives, the lack of a clear remit, deficiencies in performance management and ineffective leadership. Employers through SSCs are empowered to introduce measures, such as levies and licences to practise, where a clear majority in that sector support it.

Box 2: A demand-led system

The Review's analysis shows that previous approaches to delivering skills have been too 'supply driven', based on the Government planning supply to meet ineffectively articulated employer demand. This approach has a poor track record – it has not proved possible for employers and individuals to collectively articulate their needs or for provision to be effectively planned to meet them. Employers are confused by the plethora of advisory, strategic and planning bodies they are asked to input to. Under a planned system, the incentives are for providers to continue doing what they have done in the past so long as that meets the requirements of planning, rather than responding flexibly as demand changes. As a result, less than 10 per cent of employer training is in further education colleges.

Recent reforms in England have attempted to develop a more 'demand-led' system, responding to demand rather than trying to plan supply. Train to Gain provides flexible training, designed to meet the needs of employers and employees. Providers only receive funding if they effectively meet the needs of their customers. The Employer Training Pilots show that this approach leads to provision that better reflects the needs of consumers, increasing relevance, higher completion rates and value for money.

The Review has concluded that this sort of approach must be embedded across the system so that providers only receive funding as they attract customers, rather than receiving a block grant based upon supply-side estimates of expected demand. Building a demand-led system is the only way in which to increase employer and individual investment in skills and ensure that increased investment delivers economically valuable skills.

---

24   Employers, individuals and the Government all invest significantly in skills improvements. In England, employers spend around £2.4 billion on direct course costs and up to £17.4 billion in total, excluding the wages of employees. Employer investment in skills varies significantly by type of employee, type of employer and sector of the economy. Training by employers is disproportionately focused on highly-skilled workers, who are five times more likely to be trained at work than low skill workers. Around one third of firms do no training at all, and this varies between 50 per cent of employers in some sectors to just under 5 per cent in the best performing sectors.

25   The Government in England invests around £12 billion on adult skills each year, of which around £4.5 billion is on further education (FE), including work-based learning, and £7.4 billion on higher education (HE). These are the overall costs of tuition, learner support and capital. Individuals will pay £1.35 billion per annum through the new variable tuition fees, on top of the existing £0.9 billion per annum income from standard fees.

26   However, the combined level of investment compares poorly by international standards. Although the overall proportion of adults trained is relatively high (61 per cent), only 19 per cent of adults in the UK report contributing any of their own funding towards education and training, compared with an OECD average of 37 per cent. In addition funding for higher education in the UK from both public and private sources is low by international standards – less than one half that in the USA and 40 per cent lower than in Sweden.

Skills and employment   27   The Review has found that the skills and employment systems, which should work in tandem to improve people's job chances, are disjointed. Out of work support is not joined up with in work support. There are no effective links between someone moving into work from the New Deal and in work support such as Train to Gain that can help them stay in work and progress. Current skills and employment services have different aims, which means that delivery can be complex with an array of agencies trying to give help and advice to people. As a result, individuals do not receive the support they need and are unsure how and where to access it.

28   The key employment objective of the Department for Work and Pensions (DWP) is to increase the employment rate over the economic cycle. It has translated this into operational targets for Jobcentre Plus to help a certain number of people into work each year, with a focus on disadvantaged groups. Welfare to Work providers are also rewarded if their clients are still in work after 13 weeks. The short-term focus moves attention away from pre-work interventions that might improve the sustainability of employment, as well as creating little incentive to build links with in-work support that might improve retention. Two-thirds of Jobseekers' Allowance claims are repeat ones.

Skills projections for 2020

29   History tells us that no one can predict with any accuracy future occupational needs. The Review is clear that skill demands will increase at every single level. Better skills will be needed at higher levels to drive leadership, management and innovation – these are key drivers of productivity growth. Intermediate skills must be improved to implement investment and innovation. Basic skills are essential for people to be able to adapt to change. People lacking basic skills will be most at risk of exclusion in a global economy.

30   Improving the skills of young people, while essential, cannot be the sole solution to achieving world class skills. Improvements in attainment of young people can only deliver a small part of what is necessary because they comprise a small proportion of the overall workforce. Demographic change means that there will be smaller numbers of young people flowing into the workforce towards 2020.

31   More than 70 per cent of the 2020 working age population are already over the age of 16. As the global economy changes and working lives lengthen with population ageing, adults will increasingly need to update their skills in the workforce. There is a pressing need to raise the rates of skills improvements among adults – the UK cannot reach a world class ambition by 2020 without this.

32   The Government and Devolved Administrations have extremely demanding targets already in place to improve skills across the UK, for young people and adults and across all skill levels. These will be difficult to achieve and must not be taken for granted. Even if these targets are met, the Review has found that the UK will still fail to significantly improve its relative position by 2020, lagging behind key comparator nations with deficits across all skill levels:

- 4 million people will still lack functional literacy skills, and over 6 million will lack functional numeracy skills;
- the UK will be 15th out of 30 OECD countries in low skills, with 11 per cent of those aged over 25 still lacking the equivalent of a basic school leaving qualification, treble that of the best performing OECD countries;

- 13th in intermediate skills, with 46 per cent of those aged over 25 qualified to this level, less than in Germany, New Zealand and Finland among others; and

- 13th in terms of those aged over 25 who have attained high qualifications, still lagging behind key comparators such as the USA, Canada, Sweden and Japan.

33   This continuing shortfall will have profound implications for the UK economy and society, constraining prosperity, business ability to compete, and individual pay and job prospects. To succeed in the new global economy, the UK must raise its sights and aim for world class skills. This will require a new shared national mission, moving beyond the old distinction between voluntarism and compulsion, forging a new compact between the Government, employers, trades unions and individuals.

A NATIONAL AMBITION FOR WORLD CLASS SKILLS

34   The Review has concluded that the UK must commit itself to a world class skills base in order to secure prosperity and fairness in the new global economy. The Review recommends moving the UK into the top eight in the world at each skill level by 2020, achieving the top quartile in the OECD.

35   The Review's analysis shows that achieving world class skills will require the UK to commit to achieving by 2020:[10]

- **95 per cent of adults to have functional literacy and numeracy** (basic skills) up from 85 per cent literacy and 79 per cent numeracy in 2005; more than trebling projected rates of improvement to achieve a total of 7.4 million adult attainments over the period;

- **exceeding 90 per cent of the adult population qualified to at least Level 2**, with a commitment to achieving world class levels as soon as feasible, currently projected to be 95 per cent. An increase from 69 per cent in 2005; a total of 5.7 million adult attainments over the period;

- **shifting the balance of intermediate skills from Level 2 to Level 3.** Improving the esteem, quantity and quality of intermediate skills. Boosting the number of Apprentices to 500,000 by 2020; a total of 4 million adult Level 3 attainments over the period; and

- **world class high skills, exceeding 40 per cent of the adult population** qualified to Level 4 and above, up from 29 per cent in 2005, with a commitment to continue progression. Widening the drive to improve the UK's high skills to encompass the whole working-age population, including 18-30 year olds; a total of 5.5 million attainments over the period. Increase focus on Level 5 and above skills.

36   These are stretching ambitions, more than doubling the projected rate of attainment in many cases. They are more coherent than the current set of targets: focused on outcomes, measuring attainment rather than participation and covering the whole adult population rather than subsets. Crucially, however, these ambitions will not deliver economic benefits unless they are based on economically valuable skills that are effectively used in the workplace.

---

[10] Adults means aged 19 to State Pension age.

The impact of world class skills

37   The Government is committed to increasing the share of GDP devoted to education over the lifetime of this Parliament. Spending on skills will benefit as a result of this commitment. The level of ambition set out in this report will require additional investment by the State, employers and individuals. The Review recognises that greater efficiency in delivery, economies of scale and rationalisation in the skills landscape should reduce these costs.

38   This report recommends the optimal level of skills in the economy. The Review estimates that additional annual investment in skills up to Level 3 will need to rise to around £1.5 - £2 billion by 2020 if we are to achieve world class status at basic and intermediate levels. In addition, increased investment is required in higher education to achieve world class status. Uncertainties over HE participation data and unstable trends across much of the OECD, make it problematic to provide accurate costings for world class levels. There will be a review of funding arrangements for HE in 2009.

39   It is vital that the necessary reforms and capacity are in place to make best use of any additional investment, for example, to ensure that the additional qualifications are economically valuable. Increasing investment should be phased in carefully over time to ensure that value for money is maintained.

Balance of responsibility 40   The costs of raised ambitions must be shared between government, employers and individuals. Government investment in skills should be focused on ensuring everyone has the opportunity to build a basic platform of skills, tackling market failures and targeting help where it is needed most. There are key market failures at all skill levels, but these impact most at the bottom end. The Review recommends a much clearer financial balance of responsibility, based on clear principles of Government funding to be targeted at market failure and responsibility shared according to economic benefit. To meet additional investment this means:

- the Government should provide the bulk of funding for basic skills and the platform of skills for employability, with employers cooperating to ensure employees are able to achieve these skills;

- for higher intermediate skills (Level 3) employers and individuals should make a much higher contribution, in the order of at least 50 per cent; and

- at Level 4 and above, individuals and employers should pay the bulk of the additional costs as they will benefit most.

41   An outstanding question for Government is to translate these principles into funding formulae, in England for Train to Gain, Learning Accounts and university tuition fees. Where the Government does invest, funding must meet employers' and individuals' needs, within this framework of responsibilities.

'The prize' 42   The Review has estimated the enormous benefits that achieving this ambition would bring for the UK. The prize means more economic prosperity and increased social justice. It would deliver a possible net benefit of at least £80 billion over 30 years, an annual average of £2.5 billion. This would be driven by increased productivity and improved employment. The rate of productivity growth would increase by at least 10 per cent, helping to close the UK's productivity gap and leaving the average worker producing £1,800 more output each year by 2020 than would otherwise be the case.

43 The employment rate would grow 10 per cent more quickly than projected, with at least an additional 200,000 people into work by 2020, helping to move towards the ambition of an 80 per cent employment rate. People will have a fairer chance to progress, there will be less social deprivation and positive wider impacts on health, crime and social cohesion.

Delivering world class skills

Young people **44** If the UK is to achieve a world class skills base, it must aim for world class attainment among young people. It is unacceptable in the 21st century in the fifth richest economy in the world that young people should leave school unable to read, write and add up. Yet over one in six young people in England do.[11] The UK must avoid a new generation of people leaving school without basic skills.

14-19 reform **45** Despite recent improvements, the UK's post-16 participation in education and training is below the OECD average. At age 17, 83 per cent are enrolled in education and training, compared to more than 90 per cent in the best performing countries. International evidence suggests that parity of esteem of the vocational route and a smoothing of the current break point at age 16 are needed to achieve world-leading levels of post-16 participation in education and training. The new specialised Diplomas in England are critical to increasing participation in education and training for all young people.

46 The 14 – 19 Reform Programme must successfuly deliver a fully integrated 14 – 19 phase, including curriculum, funding and financial support; and must ensure appropriate stretch and breadth in A levels. The 2008 Review of progress as set out in the 14 – 19 White Paper published in February, 2005 will be important in identifying what more can be done to achieve their objectives. Once the Government is on track to successfully deliver Diplomas, with rising participation at age 17 and significant improvement in the OECD rankings, it should implement a change in the law, so that all young people must remain in full or part-time education or workplace training up to the age of 18.

47 Participation in higher education has increased significantly over the last decade so that around 42 per cent of young people now participate in higher education, driving a welcome increase in the proportion of highly skilled workers. However, access to university is extremely inequitable and the correlation between the chances of going to university and parental income have strengthened in recent years. Far too many young people who have the ability to go university are unable to do so because of their background. To tackle this situation will require firm Government action to raise aspirations across society so that those with the ability expect to go to university no matter what their background. It will require continuing the current trend so that standards in schools in the poorest areas rise to match those in the richest areas. And it will require firm action by the regulatory body, the Office for Fair Access.

48 For the benefits of world class skills to be realised, the Review recommends the following principles underpin their delivery:

- **shared responsibility.** Employers, individuals and the Government must increase investment and action. Employers and individuals should contribute most where they derive the greatest private returns. Government investment must focus on building a basic platform of skills for all, tackling market failures and targeting help where it is needed most;

---

[11] *Skills for Life Survey, DfES,* 2003.

- focus on economically valuable skills. Skill developments must provide real returns for individuals, for employers and for society at large. Where possible, skills should be portable to deliver mobility in the labour market for individuals and employers;

- demand-led skills. The skills system must meet the needs of individuals and employers. Vocational skills must be demand-led rather than centrally planned;

- adapt and respond. No one can accurately predict future demand for particular skill types. The framework must adapt and respond to future market needs; and

- build on existing structures. Don't always chop and change. Instead, improve the performance of the current structures through simplification and rationalisation, stronger performance management and clearer remits. Continuity is important.

A new partnership **49** Since 1945, debate has polarised around whether government needs to regulate to increase employer investment in training. The Review recommends a new partnership, building on the success of Train to Gain in England, that meets the new challenges the UK faces through common action. In practice, this means:

- Government, investing more, focusing on the least skilled. Ensuring that the education system delivers a highly-skilled flow into the workforce. Creating a framework to ensure employers and individuals drive the skills system so it delivers economically valuable skills. Being prepared to act on market failures, targeting help where it is needed most. Regulate if necessary and with care to reach the UK's skills ambitions.

- employers, to increase their investment in skills to raise productivity, wherever possible increasing investment in portable, accredited training. Ensuring that the skills system delivers economically valuable skills by effectively influencing the system. Pledging to support their low-skilled employees to reach at least a first, full Level 2. Introducing sectoral measures such as levies, where a majority of employers in the sector agree; and

- individuals, raising their aspirations and awareness. Demanding more of themselves and their employers. Investing more in their own skills development.

A DEMAND-LED SKILLS SYSTEM

50 To achieve a skills system that adds economic value, the Review recommends a simplified demand-led skills system with employers and individuals having a strong and coherent voice.

Demand-led funding **51** Route all adult vocational skills public funding in England, apart from community learning, through Train to Gain and Learner Accounts by 2010. The (LSC) Learning and Skills Council has made good progress in streamlining its operations. Going forward, the Review recommends further significant streamlining of the LSC and its working relationships with other partners. The LSC will continue to manage Train to Gain, Learner Accounts, Apprenticeships, process funding and ensure effective provider competition. There are some programmes which cannot be made wholly demand-led such as those for adults with disabilities. However, as far as possible, funding should be routed through mechanisms which put effective purchasing power in the hands of customers. This will give training providers a real incentive to deliver the skills that employers and individuals need, flexibly and responsively. If providers do not deliver, they will not receive public funding. This will ensure that providers deliver training that directly reflects demand from local employers and individuals. This approach is an opportunity for training providers, including FE colleges, to raise their game, to compete on merit and to secure healthy growth. The Devolved Administrations should consider how best to ensure that provision is effectively led by the needs of employers and individuals.

Commission for Employment and Skills

52 Strengthen the employer voice, through the creation of a dynamic, employer-led Commission for Employment and Skills to deliver greater leadership and influence, within a national framework of individual rights and responsibilities. This will rationalise the existing system by merging and streamlining the Sector Skills Development Agency (SSDA) and the National Employment Panel (NEP), both operating across the UK, into a new organisation. In England, the Commission will also replace the Ministerially-led Skills Alliance and will ensure better integration of the current, disjointed Employment and Skills services. It will be responsible for:

- reporting on progress towards the UK's world class ambitions; scrutinising system objectives and delivery; recommending policy and operational improvements and innovations; and

- SSCs and a network of Employment and Skills Boards.

53 Establishing the employer-led Commission, will help to 'depoliticise' the skills agenda by securing a broad political and stakeholder consensus for the UK's world-class ambitions for 2020 and beyond. This will allow the UK to take a clearer, long-term view of its employment and skills needs towards 2020. Several Cabinet members will have an interest in the Commission. The Review suggests that it reports to the Prime Minister, or the Chancellor of the Exchequer supported by the Secretaries of State for Education and Skills, Work and Pensions and Trade and Industry. The Commission will also report to senior Ministers in Scotland, Wales and Northern Ireland. It will be chaired by an eminent business leader and comprise senior, high profile figures, including the Director General of the CBI and the General Secretary of the TUC. It will also include independent members, for example, relevant academics and representatives from the voluntary sector.

Sector Skills Councils

54 Increase employer engagement and investment in skills – building on international evidence of successful sectoral approaches in Australia and the Netherlands and examples of excellence from existing SSCs. Reform, relicense and empower SSCs to focus on:

- taking the lead role in developing occupational standards, approving vocational qualifications;

- taking the lead role in collating and communicating sectoral labour market data;

- raising employer engagement, demand and investment; and

- considering collective employer action to address specific sector skills needs.

55 This clearer remit will make it easier to judge whether SSCs are performing effectively. The increased responsibility SSCs will have under this more focused remit, particularly their lead role in qualifications, will give employers a much greater incentive to engage with their SSC and performance manage it from the bottom up. The Commission will performance manage SSCs from the top down, relicensing those that are failing.

56   For vocational qualifications, only those approved by SSCs should qualify for public funding. Ensuring that only those qualifications approved by employers attract public funding will lead to a simplified qualification system, with fewer qualifications overall and only qualifications delivering economically valuable skills, attracting a return in the labour market, receiving public funding. This would apply to funding for work-based learning qualifications. SSC approved qualifications will be overseen by the QCA operating a risk-based, light-touch regulatory regime. There are currently over 22,000 qualifications which present a confusing picture for employers and individuals. SSCs should develop a short list of valid qualifications, with a very significant reduction in the overall number by 2008.

Brokerage **57**   The Review recommends that Train to Gain brokers are tasked to work with a full range of employers while retaining their focus on 'harder to reach' firms. The LSC's National Employer Service should be expanded to provide a more effective advisory and brokerage service to larger firms.

58   Together, these reforms will deliver a simplified, economically valuable skills system driven by demand rather than central planning. This will transform the incentives of providers, requiring them to actively react to employers and individuals, rather than recruiting students to meet supply-side targets.

EMPLOYER ENGAGEMENT

Basic platform of skills

59   Of the 11.5 million adults currently lacking a Level 2 qualification, almost 7 million are in employment. Level 2 broadly equates to 5 GCSEs A*-C or equivalent. Increasingly, Level 2 is the minimum platform of skills required for employment and business competitiveness, as global economic changes reduce the employment opportunities for the unskilled. Exceeding 90 per cent of adults having a Level 2 qualification, achieving 95 per cent as soon as feasible, will require the commitment and sustained action on behalf of Government, employers and individuals.

60   The most recent and successful approach to delivering this platform of skills to employees is through Train to Gain, delivering training flexibly and tailored to meet the needs of employers and employees. The Government has committed to increase funding to Train to Gain to £1billion by 2010. The Review's analysis, in Chart 4, shows that, despite the expected success of Train to Gain in England, it will be extremely stretching for the UK to move from the 70 per cent qualified to at least Level 2 today to world class by 2020.

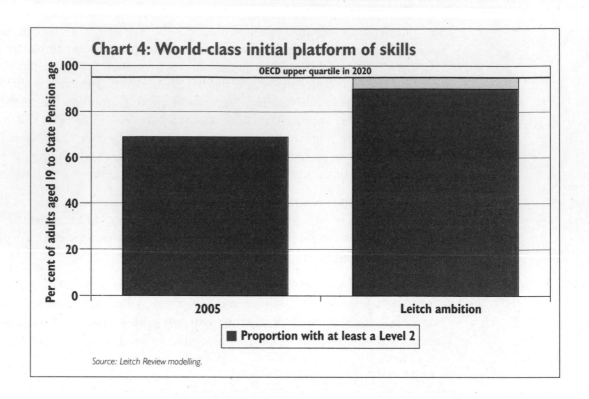

Chart 4: World-class initial platform of skills

OECD upper quartile in 2020

Per cent of adults aged 19 to State Pension age

2005   Leitch ambition

■ Proportion with at least a Level 2

Source: Leitch Review modelling.

The Pledge **61** In a recent initiative in Wales, over 10 per cent of employees are already covered by a Basic Skills Pledge by their employers, guaranteeing them access to training in work. The Review recommends that the Government work with employer representative organisations to support and encourage all employers in the UK in making a skills pledge building on recent experience in Wales. The skills pledge would be a specific promise to the workforce that every eligible employee would be helped to gain basic skills and a level 2 qualification. A major campaign, with public and private employer champions, would encourage employers to make a 'Pledge' that every relevant employee be enabled to gain basic and Level 2 equivalent skills – with tuition costs from the Government and time allowances at work. Government should consider giving small employers wage compensation for these time allowances. With key employers leading the way, the Review sees the potential of mass employer engagement with the 'Pledge' to deliver significant early progress against the world class objectives at Basic Skills and Level 2.

Entitlement to **62** In 2010, the Government and the Commission should review progress in the light of **workplace** take-up and employer delivery on their 'Pledges'. If the improvement rate is insufficient, **training at** Government should introduce a statutory entitlement to workplace training for individuals **Level 2** without a full Level 2 qualification, delivered in England through Train to Gain. The entitlement will need to be carefully designed so that it minimises bureaucracy and avoids being overly prescriptive. It must be designed in consultation with employers and trades unions.

63 Investors in People (IiP) can engage employers in developing the skills of their employees to enhance business performance, recognising achievement through a common standard. The Government should, in consultation with the Commission and leading employers, review the remit of IiP, to consider how IiPUK and its products, including the Standard itself and the new 'profile' tool, should be reshaped to support delivery of the Review's ambition.

Intermediate skills

64   Higher intermediate skills are increasingly critical to the success of business, with high private returns. The Review recommends shifting the balance of intermediate skills to Level 3, more than doubling the rate of attainment of Level 3 skills by adults. Apprenticeships are a crucial method of delivering work-focused intermediate skills. After a steep decline since the 1970s, more than 250,000 people are now participating in Apprenticeships.[12] However, the completion rate of the full framework is poor at 53 per cent[13] compared to 70 per cent in Train to Gain. Many employers complain that the Apprenticeship process is complex and bureaucratic. Government must take action to improve completion rates.

Apprenticeships 65   The Government must work with employers to deliver a major improvement in the UK's intermediate skills base. The Review recommends that, as with vocational qualifications, employers should drive the content of Apprenticeships through their SSC. This will ensure that Apprenticeships are relevant to employers and high quality. SSA should include clear commitments and targets, including for the number of Apprenticeships, for increased employer achievement of intermediate and higher skills. The Government should work with the Commission, SSCs and LSC to dramatically increase the number of Apprenticeships in the UK to 500,000 by 2020, with skills brokers engaging with individual employers to demonstrate business benefits.

66   The Government should build on the success of the Apprenticeship route, expanding it to become a pathway which is open to every suitably qualified 16-19 year old. It will always be a voluntary matter for employers to choose whether to offer apprenticeship places. SSCsand skills brokers should work with employers to achieve the necessary increase in the supply of high quality places for young people and adults. As a result of this shared action, **the Government should consider creating a new entitlement as resources allow so that every young person with the right qualifications should be able to take up an Apprenticeship place.**

High skills

67   A highly-skilled workforce drives innovation, leadership and management, enabling businesses to compete in the global economy. Ensuring that high skills are of world class quality and relevance to the economy is just as important as determining the quantity of people that should be qualified to these levels. The Review's world class ambition requires increased engagement and investment from employers with higher education, to drive management, innovation and workforce development. In 2009, the Government will establish an independent review, working with the Office of Fair Access, to report to Parliament on all aspects of the new variable fees and student funding arrangements based on the first three years operation of the policy.

68   **The Review's recommendation is to exceed 40 per cent of the adult population with Level 4 or above skills, widening the drive to improve the UK's high skills to encompass the whole working-age population.** Changing the targets away from the sole focus on young people aged 18-30 will transform the incentives of HE providers to work with employers, delivering a step change in liaison between employers and higher education institutions. **To further embed these incentives, the Review recommends that a portion of higher education funding be delivered through a similar demand-led mechanism as Train to Gain in England, contributing to both young and adult HE attainment levels. Government funding should also be used to stimulate greater private investment, for example through the co-financing of university research chairs by employers and the Government.**

---

[12] *Departmental Report*, DfES, 2006.

[13] *Raising our game: our annual statement of priorities*, LSC, October 2006.

Management and leadership 69   Skills must be effectively used for their benefits to be fully realised. Many small employers need support to ensure that they have sufficient management and leadership ability to deploy skills effectively. They also need access to impartial advice so that they can invest effectively in skills that will benefit their business. Employers are already investing a lot in improving management skills, though evidence shows it is less than elsewhere in Europe.[14] Over one half of CBI employers cite improving management and leadership skills as the most significant factor contributing to competitiveness. Over 30,000 firms have signed up to IiP standards, demonstrating a commitment to improving management.

70   To further improve the UK's management and leadership, **the Review recommends that SSCs and skills brokers drive up employer investment in management skills by employers. It recommends that the successful Department for Education and Skills (DfES) Leadership and Management funding programme for small and medium size enterprises (SMEs) be extended to firms with between 10 and 20 employees so that smaller businesses can benefit from it. There is a good case for the current Leadership and Management Advisory Panel to report to the Commission.**

EMBEDDING A CULTURE OF LEARNING

71   Individuals must play their part in a shared mission for world class skills. This will require a culture of learning to be fully embedded across society, so that all groups are able to invest in the development of their skills, driving a step change in participation in skills improvements. Changing culture will be a generational task, but a change in behaviour can start today.

Inequalities at school 72   The Review has found that inequalities in aspiration by adults drive inequalities in attainment for their children at school. This creates a cycle of disadvantage that locks generations of the same family into persistent poverty. It perpetuates the number of young people unable to read, write and add up and who drop out of school at 16, spending teenage years not in education, employment or training (NEET). This cycle needs to be broken by raising the aspirations of parents and children and standards in all schools.

A new offer for adults 73   The Review recommends a new offer to adults to help increase a culture of learning across the country, ensuring everyone gets the help they need to get on in life:

- **raising aspiration and awareness.** A new and sustained national campaign to raise career aspirations and awareness of the benefits from learning, backed by local outreach activity. Increasing the appetite and the opportunity to learn;

- **making informed choices.** In England, a new universal adult careers service, learning from those elsewhere in the UK, providing a universal source of labour market focused, accessible careers advice for adults;

- **increasing choice.** Giving individuals choice and control by entitling them to a Learner Account, learning from the schemes in Wales and Scotland, that they can use to pay towards the accredited learning of their choice; and

- **ensuring individuals can afford to learn.** Financial support based on the principles of clarity and targeting to help those who need it most. In England, a new Skills Development Fund, subsuming the Learner Support Fund, will tackle the immediate barriers for those wanting to improve their basic and Level 2 skills.

---

[14] *Leadership and management in the UK: Raising our ambition*, The Leadership and Management Advisory Panel, Submission to the Leitch Review, October 2006.

74   These reforms will raise awareness and aspiration across society. They will ensure individuals have the help and support they need to get a good job, build their career and deliver economic security in a changing global economy.

INTEGRATING EMPLOYMENT AND SKILLS SERVICES

75   In Budget 2006, the Chancellor commissioned the Leitch Review to consider how to better integrate skills and employment services. Skills, and particularly qualifications, offer individuals the flexibility to advance, change jobs and careers. The UK has significant problems with job retention at basic entry levels: around two thirds of all Jobseeker's Allowance (JSA) claims each year are repeat claims.

An integrated service 76   The Review proposes a new integrated employment and skills service, drawing together existing services such as Jobcentre Plus and the new adult careers service. It will offer universal access to work-focused careers advice, basic skills screening, job placement and links to in-work training. Common objectives and aligned incentives will drive delivery which will be monitored by the Commission and Employment and Skills Boards. This will ensure individuals receive effective support to get into work, stay in employment and progress. Delivering this will require:

- **a new single objective of sustainable employment and progression opportunities.** Meeting this aim will require all involved in such services, from DfES and DWP, the LSC and Jobcentre Plus, to front line staff and colleges, to change their work practices;

- as stated above, **a new universal adult careers service, providing labour market focused careers advice for all adults.** The new careers service will deliver advice in a range of locations, including co-location with Jobcentre Plus, creating a national network of one-stop shops for careers and employment advice;

- **a network of employer-led Employment and Skills Boards,** reporting to the Commission. Their role will be to engage local employers, articulate local labour market needs, scrutinise local services and recommend improvements in integrating labour market and training support. Engaging local employers will improve the matching of work-ready applicants to sustainable jobs, including the disadvantaged. This network will rationalise and build on successful city, employer coalition and regional models; and

- **a much greater role for basic skills training in the benefit system,** including a new programme to screen all those returning to benefits within one year, and better incentivising benefit claimants to improve their basic skills.

77   These reforms will deliver an integrated service to help individuals get into the labour market and progress, equipping front-line workers with the tools they need to help people build economic security in a changing global economy. They will ensure that all services are incentivised to help people stay in work and progress, better linking services together and ensuring that support is not cut off when people move into work.

IMPACT

78   Together, these recommendations will deliver world-class skills and have a positive impact on the UK's economic and social welfare performance. The impact in particular areas is listed below.

Individual awareness 79   All individuals will have a greater awareness of the value of skills development and easier access to the opportunities available to them.

Workless people 80   People who are out of work will receive much more targeted, comprehensive help and support, focused on both their short and long-term prospects. Co-locating services is more convenient for customers. It opens up easy access to both employment and careers advice to all benefit claimants, from the unemployed to lone parents and those with health problems and disabilities. Individuals will be screened for basic skills needs at the start of their claim, rather than after 6 months. Where basic skills needs are the key barrier to work, they will be referred to flexible training, alongside job search activity. On finding work, they will be referred to training through Train to Gain. Training will be more relevant to the needs of the local labour market as a result of the input from Employment and Skills Boards and SSCs.

81   People who struggle to stay in employment will receive a full Skills Health Check at the start of their claim, which will shape their Back to Work Plan. They will also receive additional in-work support. Individuals will be able to access labour market advice from the new adult careers service operating 'virtually' and in a number of locations, including a one-stop shop within Jobcentre Plus. Motivation will be increased through a high profile national awareness campaign, backed up by local activity.

Low-skilled workers 82   Low-skilled workers will have much greater awareness of the benefits of training and know where to access relevant careers advice. The worker's employer may pledge to upskill all eligible employees or be advised by a local Train to Gain broker. Within the employer's training plan, the individual could access support for workplace training to their first, full Level 2 qualification. The individual is more likely to experience a positive wage return if their employer supports the training and it takes place in the workplace. After 2010, if the legal entitlement to workplace training is invoked, the individual may qualify for the statutory right to ask their employer to train towards a full Level 2 qualification within the workplace.

83   An individual can use their Learner Account to act on the advice of the new national careers service. They will find out in advance what their financial support entitlement is, helping them to make an informed decision about the type and length of course they undertake. People will be more in control of their learning.

Skilled workers 84   Skilled workers will benefit from greater opportunities to develop themselves and their careers. Both employers and individuals will invest more in training. Train to Gain brokers will be in contact with an increasing proportion of employers. Discussions will take place with managers and owners about the best training for their organisations. This will include the offer for match-funded Level 3 training, management training or Level 4 courses such as Foundation degrees. More adult Apprenticeships will be available for those individuals and their employers who wish to fill skill gaps.

85   There are more options for employees who wish to develop their career away from their existing employer or alongside their current jobs. All people in the UK will be able to access an adult careers service. This will have up-to-date information on courses, financial support and also on the types of qualifications that have real value in the workplace. Individuals will be able to access training with real economic value and do so through their new Learner Account.

SMEs 86   More small and medium employers will have access to Train to Gain brokers to advise on their training needs and on public subsidies available. SMEs will benefit from more relevant, economically valuable skills delivered through flexible provision. Employers with between 10 and 250 employees will be able to access a grant for management and leadership training. This will help them to maximise the bottom line impact of their employees' skills development. Employment and Skills Boards will scrutinise the functioning of local careers and employment information to ensure that it better reflects employer needs. Employers will be able to fill their vacancies more easily.

Employers 87   Employers, both public and private, will have more influence over the skills strategy within a simplified system through the collective voice of the Commission. They will approve the qualifications that are publicly funded and control vocational content through their SSC. Employers with high quality in-house training schemes can apply to an SSC to have their training accredited, in a streamlined process regulated by the QCA. Employers will benefit from having more access to flexible, unitised qualifications across all skill levels to upskill and motivate their employees.

88   Large employers will have access to an expanded, specialised skills broker service to advise on how to improve their bottom line through investing in skills across all levels; to advise on the public funding available and signpost suitable training providers. They will have greater incentives to invest in high quality training. There will be more public funding for adult Apprenticeships and other Level 3 qualifications. Universities will be more responsive to the needs of large employers who want to deliver degrees in the workplace or bespoke training for highly-skilled workers, including management and leadership training.

Improved labour 89   Skills deficiencies will reduce. Upskilling will increase and ensure improved labour
supply supply to a higher standard of competence.

CONCLUSION

90   The UK's skills profile has improved markedly against historical standards and the system is aiming to deliver stretching targets. In international terms, the scale of the challenge faced by the UK remains daunting. The UK needs a dramatic step change in its skills performance if it is to improve growth, productivity and social justice in a rapidly changing global economy. The Review has set out a radical and compelling vision. It recommends that the UK commit to world class skills, doubling projected rates of attainment. The costs of achieving this must be shared fairly. But they are dwarfed by the benefits – increased productivity, employment and social justice.

91   Achieving world class skills will require shared action between the Government, employers and individuals. The Review recommends employer commitments to increase investment in intermediate and high skills. At the lower end, the Review recommends a joint Government and employer programme to train all eligible employees to a full Level 2 qualification. If this shared action does not meet the scale of the challenge by 2010, a statutory entitlement to workplace to Level 2 training should be introduced.

92   The Review has set out proposals to rationalise the skills system, placing employers more at its heart and reducing supply-side planning of skills provision. The number of bodies involved in skills delivery and employer voice will be significantly reduced, simplifying employer engagement. The roles and responsibilities of remaining bodies will be clarified.

93   The Review recognises the need to energise individuals, building a culture of learning by raising awareness. A new, universal adult careers service will be central to this, sitting alongside reforms to give learners clarity about financial support entitlements.

94   The result of these reforms will be a step change in skills development. Skills will be one of the UK's key strengths, rather than a significant weakness. The UK will be on a higher trajectory toward increased productivity, growth and social justice, meeting the challenge of increased prosperity and fairness in the new global economy.

NEXT STEPS

95   This policy framework will deliver world class skills, given the right investment and delivery reform. However, this is not a detailed blueprint for implementation. Government should now consider these recommendations and decide the next steps of the journey.

96   The Devolved Administrations in Northern Ireland, Scotland and Wales should now consider the Review's recommended policy framework in the context of differing circumstances in those countries and their contribution for delivering world class, economically valuable skills.

THE INCREASING IMPORTANCE OF SKILLS

Chapter summary

The Leitch Review was established to consider the UK's long-term skills needs, in order to maximise productivity, economic growth and social justice. The UK is in a strong economic position, with 14 years of unbroken growth and world class employment. Despite this, the UK has a significant productivity gap with many comparator countries. The employment rates of disadvantaged groups have risen significantly, but remain below the average. There have been significant reductions in child poverty, but income inequality remains relatively high and social mobility low. Skills are a vital determinant of prosperity, driving national productivity and employment, businesses' ability to take advantage of new opportunities and individuals' career prospects.

The Review has found that fundamental changes underway in the global economy mean that the future prosperity of advanced economies increasingly depends on their skills bases. Emerging economies are growing rapidly. Technological change and global migration flows are increasing. These changes are breaking down the barriers between what can and cannot be traded and increasing skills requirements across the economy. The prosperity of advanced economies increasingly depends on their skills. Just as being at the forefront of the Industrial Revolution determined prosperity in the previous century, so making the most of these changes through the skills of the people will determine prosperity in this century.

Skills are also a key determinant of fairness. In the new global economy, people's economic security cannot come from trying to protect particular jobs, holding back the tide of change. Instead it comes from enabling people to adapt to change, and this relies upon equipping people with the skills to be flexible and take advantage of new opportunities. In the new century, improving and updating skills is the best way to help people make the most of change. To achieve world class prosperity and fairness, the UK must have world class skills.

The following chapters set out the Review's recommendation of a shared national commitment to world class skills, and the respective roles of government, employers, trades unions and individuals.

1.1   The Leitch Review was established in December 2004 to consider the skills profile the UK should aim to achieve by 2020 in order to maximise growth, productivity and social justice. The UK must aim to improve its prosperity and fairness in a rapidly changing global economy. The Review has found that these changes are decisively increasing the importance of skills. Skills are an increasingly central driver of productivity, employment and fairness. The UK must achieve a world class skills base if it is to improve its prosperity and fairness in the new global economy.

THE INCREASING IMPORTANCE OF SKILLS

1.2   The Review's interim report, *Skills in the UK: The long-term challenge*, showed that the UK remains in a strong economic position, with world class employment levels and the longest sustained period of economic growth on record.[1] However, the Review has found that the UK should be doing better and must raise its game as the global economy changes. Improvements in the UK's skills base are key to this.

---

[1] *Skills in the UK: The long-term challenge*, HM Treasury, 2005.

> **Box 1.1: What do we mean by skills?**
>
> There are a large number of different types of skills and they can be split into a number of different categories. Basic skills, such as literacy and numeracy, and generic skills, such as team working and communication, are applicable in most jobs. Specific skills tend to be less transferable between occupations. Most occupations use a mix of different types of skills and within each skill there are different levels of ability. For skills to benefit the economy, they must be economically valuable. That is, they must benefit individuals through higher wages and businesses through improved productivty.
>
> There is no perfect measure of skills. The most common measures of skills are qualifications, although it is possible to have skills without having qualifications. On the job training in the workplace is a vital source of skills development and career progression, but often not formally recognised. The Review recognises the importance of looking at these wider definitions of skills. Qualifications help people when they need to move job and help employers judge applicants for work. According to a recent survey, the contents of the application form or CV, including qualifications gained, are the most frequently used selection method (66 per cent) by employers.[a]
>
> Qualifications can be grouped into five different levels: full Level 2 equates to five good GCSEs or their vocational equivalents, full Level 3 to two or more A Levels and Level 4 and above to degree level qualifications. Levels of literacy and numeracy tend to be based on surveys or on the proportion of people with English or Maths qualifications.
>
> [a] *Recruitment, Retention and Turnover Survey*, CIPD, 2006.

The UK economy 1.3   The UK economy has changed significantly over time. Today the service sector accounts for around three quarters of the UK economy. Almost 29 million people are employed in the UK. Of these, 3.8 million are self-employed. Small firms with less than 50 employees, excluding the self-employed, account for around one quarter of employment, with large firms (250 or more employees) accounting for 41 per cent.[2] The public sector accounts for more than 20 per cent of total employment. Improving economic prosperity will mean tackling the different challenges that the different types of employer in the UK face.

1.4   The UK's challenge is to drive greater increases in prosperity as the global economy changes fundamentally. Emerging economies, such as India and China, are growing dramatically. By 2015, China is likely to have become the third largest economy in the world.[3] Technology is rapidly breaking down the barriers between what can and cannot be traded and increasing skills requirements across the economy. The Review has found that such changes are rapidly increasing the importance of skills. The Organisation for Economic Co-operation and Development (OECD) stresses that, as emerging economies increase their supply of high skills, OECD countries would ignore the resulting pressures at great cost to their economic well-being.[4] As the global economy changes, an economy's prosperity will be driven increasingly by its skills base.

The productivity challenge

1.5   The UK's productivity – how much workers produce – has improved in recent years. Despite this, it still lags behind that of many comparator countries on most measures. Chart 1.1 shows that the average worker in France produces 20 per cent more per hour than the average UK worker. The average German worker produces 13 per cent more and the average US worker 18 per cent more.

---

[2] *Small and medium-sized enterprise statistics for the UK 2005*, Small Business Service, 2006.
[3] Based on market exchange rates. See *Long-term global economic challenges and opportunities for the UK*, HM Treasury, 2004.
[4] *Education at a glance*, OECD, 2006.

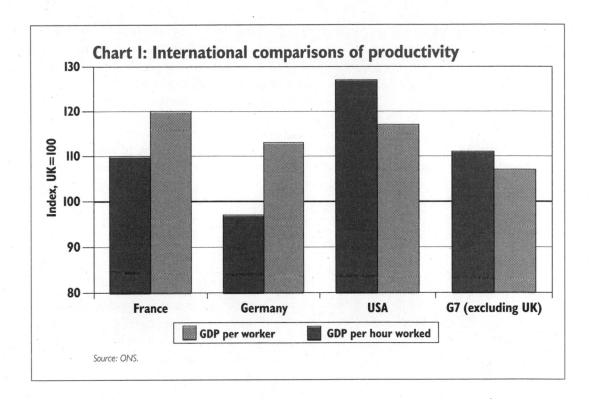

Chart I: International comparisons of productivity

Index, UK=100

Legend: GDP per worker | GDP per hour worked

Source: ONS.

1.6   There are five key drivers of productivity: competition, enterprise, innovation, investment and skills. Skills impact on productivity:

- directly, by increasing human capital in a firm or country;

- indirectly, by 'spillover' impacts on the productivity of other workers; and

- via other drivers, by encouraging greater investment and innovation.

National productivity   1.7   The Review has found that the UK's relatively poor skills base has constrained productivity and national prosperity. Evidence shows that around one fifth of the UK's productivity gap with countries such as France and Germany results from the relatively poor skills of workers in the UK – if the UK had similar skill levels as these countries, its national income would be significantly higher.[5] The extent of this productivity gap varies between sectors, regions and countries of the UK. Productivity in the East of England is more than 20 per cent higher than the UK average, while in the North East it is around 10 per cent lower. A recent study found that the utilities sector is five times more productive than the UK average, while hotels and catering are only 40 per cent as productive as the average.[6]

---

[5] *Britain's relative productivity performance: updates to 1999*, O'Mahoney and de Boer, National Institute for Economic and Social Research, 2002.

[6] *Skills for Business network: Sectoral productivity differences across the UK*, Research Report 13, Sector Skills Development Agency, 2005.

1.8 There is clear consensus that improvements in skills provide a boost to growth and are associated with higher levels of national income in the long term.[7] Analysis shows that improvements in the skills of UK workers contributed around one fifth of annual growth in the UK economy over the past 25 years.[8] Another study found a similar contribution of 0.37 percentage points to annual growth over the five years to 2000.[9] Improving skills more quickly than in the past can increase this contribution and increase economic growth.

Business productivity **1.9** Improving the skills of workers increases the productivity of businesses and helps them to compete in the global economy. Evidence clearly demonstrates that higher skills are associated with increased productivity and improved business outcomes at the firm level. The higher wages that firms are prepared to pay to workers with higher qualifications provide a measure of the impact of skills on productivity – in general, firms would not pay them higher wages if they were not more productive.

1.10 Wages are a conservative estimate of the productivity benefits of gaining skills through qualifications. Evidence shows that the productivity benefits are higher than the wage benefits. One study showed that a 5 percentage point increase in the proportion of workers trained in an industry leads to a 1.6 per cent increase in wages but a 4 per cent increase in value-added per worker – the increase in productivity was approximately double the increase in wages.[10] Similarly, recent evidence suggests that the impact of training on productivity may be double the size of the wage effect.[11]

1.11 A much fuller discussion of the evidence on the importance of skills in driving national and business productivity, both directly and indirectly, can be found in the Review's interim report.

1.12 In the new global economy, discussed more fully below, skills are an ever more important determinant of productivity, prosperity and business competitiveness. As the global economy integrates and technology breaks down the barriers between what can and cannot be traded, activities will increasingly be located according to comparative advantage. The UK's comparative advantage cannot and should not come from low labour costs alone. Instead it must come from the skills of its people. In the new global economy, the UK can only achieve world class prosperity through world class skills.

The employment challenge

1.13 The second major component of economic prosperity is the number of people in work. The UK's overall employment rate is one of the highest in the G7 at almost 75 per cent. Recent years have seen overall rises in employment, including among previously disadvantaged groups. For example, the employment rate of lone parents has risen by more than 11 percentage points since 1997.

---

[7] For a summary of the literature, see *The returns to education: a review of the empirical macroeconomic literature*, Sianesi and van Reenan, Institute for Fiscal Studies, 2002.

[8] *A quality-adjusted labour input series for the United Kingdom (1975-2002)*, Bell, Burriel-Llombart and Jones, Bank of England Working Paper 280, 2005.

[9] *Accounting growth: capital, skills and output*, Lau and Vaze, Office for National Statistics, 2002.

[10] *Who gains when workers train? Training and corporate productivity in a panel of British industries*, Dearden, Reed and van Reenan, Institute for Fiscal Studies, 2000.

[11] *The impact of training on productivity and wages: evidence from British panel data*, Dearden, Reed and van Reenan, 2005.

I.14 Despite this, 7.8 million people are economically inactive (not in or looking for work), a rate of more than 20 per cent that has fallen little over the past decade. For example, just under 2.7 million people with health problems and disabilities are out of work and claiming benefits. Many people in this group want to work. This shows there is further scope to increase employment and meet the Government's aspiration of an 80 per cent employment rate. As Chart 1.2 shows, employment among groups such as lone parents, those from ethnic minority groups and people with disabilities remain significantly below the national average, although the gap has narrowed over the past decade.

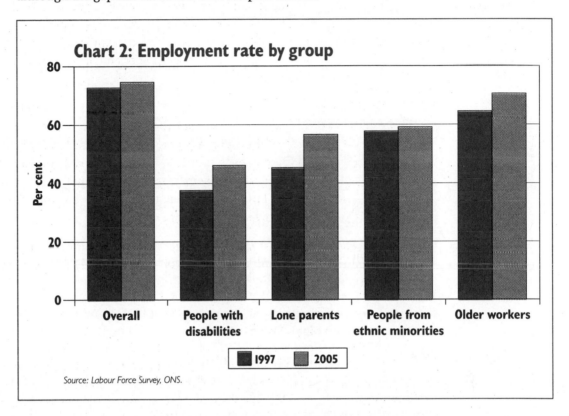

Chart 2: Employment rate by group

Source: Labour Force Survey, ONS.

I.15 Increasingly, skills are a key determinant of employment. Just under 50 per cent of those with no qualifications are in work, compared to nearly 90 per cent for those with graduate level qualifications. There is clear evidence that those with particular skills are more likely to be in work than similar people without skills. One study found that numeracy skills at Level 1, equivalent to the standard needed for a GCSE Maths at grades D-G, are associated with a 2-3 percentage point higher probability of being in employment.[12] It found that Level 1 literacy skills are associated with as much as a 10 percentage point higher probability of being in work.

I.16 As the global economy changes, skills will be an increasingly important driver of employment. Economic security will depend not on protecting particular jobs. Instead, ensuring that people are able to stay in the labour market, equipped with the skills and flexibility to find their next job and build their career, will be key to their security. The focus of welfare policy must shift from protecting people from change to ensuring people can adapt to change. A platform of skills will help people to find and stay in work. Providing opportunities to improve skills will help people advance in work. Skills are central to increasing employment, helping people stay in work and giving them the opportunities to get on in work.

---

[12] *The returns to academic, vocational and basic skills in Britain*, McIntosh, Dearden, Myck and Vignoles, Skills Task Force Research Paper 20, 2000.

THE CHANGING GLOBAL CONTEXT

1.17   The Review has found that fundamental changes underway in the global economy, combined with shifts in the structure of the UK workforce as the population ages, are dramatically increasing the importance of skills. In the future, the prosperity of economies will increasingly depend on their skills bases. Workers will have to retrain, upskill and change jobs more often during the course of longer working lives.

Global economic changes

1.18   Faster information flows and falling transport costs are breaking down geographical barriers to economic activity. Changes in technology and trade are opening up global markets and changing global patterns of production. The boundary between what can and cannot be traded is being rapidly eroded. As a result, economic activities are increasingly located according to comparative advantage. In this expanding and more deeply integrated global economy, the comparative advantage of the UK must lie in the skills of its people, rather than on low labour costs alone.

Balance of global activity   **1.19**   The rapid growth of emerging economies, including China and India, is shifting the global balance of economic activity. By 2015, China is likely to have become the third largest economy in the world, after the US and Japan.[13] This creates new markets for UK firms and provides cheaper goods for UK consumers. It also means the UK will have a decreasing share of output in the sectors in which these countries have a comparative advantage. To maintain and improve growth, the UK must manage the resulting domestic structural change, allowing workers and resources to shift to more productive and profitable activities and sectors. This structural change is contributing to the growth of high skilled jobs in the UK. To adapt to it, the UK needs more highly skilled workers.

Increasing specialisation   **1.20**   Combined with advances in information and communication technology (ICT), these changes also create new ways of producing goods and services. Different parts of the production process increasingly take place in different areas or countries, according to the comparative advantage of that area or country. While such specialisation has been most common in manufacturing, it is happening increasingly in service sector industries. For example, the financial markets, retail, communications and the media and banking sectors account for almost 40 per cent of all outsourcing.[14]

1.21   This means that, in addition to the structural changes discussed above, many types of jobs in a wide range of sectors can now be based in many different locations. The UK must make the skills of the people its key strength if it is to build a comparative advantage in the high skill, high wage jobs that will drive prosperity. While the proportion of workers with high skills in emerging economies remains extremely low, the size of countries such as India and China means that they have high absolute numbers of skilled workers. India and China together produce around 4 million graduates each year, compared to 600,000 higher level qualifications in the UK.[15]

Increasing importance of high skills   **1.22**   These changes have far reaching implications for the UK, changing the types of jobs available and the skills they require. As the global economy restructures, the success of developed countries will depend on building a flexible economy with a highly skilled workforce, which can respond quickly to change and which focuses increasingly on high

---

[13] Based on market exchange rates. See *Long-term global economic challenges and opportunities for the UK*, HM Treasury, 2004.

[14] IBM, 2004.

[15] *China Statistical Yearbook 2004*, FCO estimates and Higher Education Statistics Agency.

value-added sectors. While growth in emerging economies does not necessarily come at the expense of growth in developed countries – there are not a fixed number of jobs in the world – the UK must ensure it is a world leader in skills or risk not reaping the full benefits of high value-added industries and new technologies.

1.23   Over the past 20 years or so, the proportion of jobs requiring high skills has increased substantially, as technology and the global economy have changed. Technological change often leads to higher demand for skills and most employers that presented evidence to the Review expressed concern about shortages at intermediate and higher skill levels. Where establishments are undergoing high levels of technological change in their processes, skill needs are reported to have 'gone up a lot' for 42 per cent of jobs, compared to only 25 per cent of jobs in other establishments.[16] These changes will continue as the global economy restructures. Only if the UK is a world leader in skills can UK businesses be world leaders in the new global economy.

1.24   Skilled workers are better able to adapt quickly and effectively to change.[17] The ability of companies to absorb new technology is linked to a firm's skill composition.[18] This partly explains why the wage returns to a degree have remained broadly stable over the past decade despite large increases in the number of graduates – demand for high skill workers has risen broadly in line with their supply.[19] Projections to 2020 commissioned by the Review suggest this pattern will continue. They project a 50 per cent increase in the share of highly skilled occupations, such as managers and professionals, and a decrease in low skilled occupations, such as elementary occupations.[20]

Changing demand at the lower end   1.25   The shift in low value-added production to emerging economies does not necessarily mean that demand for relatively low skilled workers will continue to fall. Rather, the type of demand at the lower end of the labour market is shifting further towards service sector jobs, such as hospitality and personal service work.

1.26   These lower level service sector jobs require different types of skills to the more traditional low skill jobs, such as basic manufacturing, which they are replacing. In particular, they place greater emphasis on customer handling, team working and communication skills, which are essential in a service economy. Some have suggested that these shifts in the type of jobs may mean that work is polarising. The increase in the proportion of high skilled workers is leading to increased demand for less skilled workers in some service sector jobs, such as the hospitality sector. At the same time, technology may be increasingly substituting for some intermediate skill jobs, such as some craft jobs.[21]

Increasing skills within occupations   1.27   In addition to a change in the occupational structure, the skills needed within a particular occupation are also changing. Skills that were once seen as high level are increasingly seen as basic skills. The ability to use a computer is one of the most visible and widely used generic skills. The past few decades have seen a rapid expansion in the need for IT skills across all occupations and sectors. This rise has not been concentrated in traditionally high skilled jobs. Even in those occupations traditionally thought of as low skilled there has been dramatic growth in the use of IT. These changes mean that even traditionally low skilled jobs are requiring an increased level of skill – these jobs are not immune from the rising demand for skills seen elsewhere.

---

[16] *Employer perspectives survey*, Green, Mayhew and Molloy, 2003.

[17] *Education and training for manufacturing development*, Cassen and Mavrotas in *Skill development for international competitiveness*, Godfrey (ed), Institute of Development Studies, University of Sussex, 1997.

[18] *Asia's next giant: South Korea and late industrialisation*, Amsden,1989.

[19] *Further analysis of the returns to academic and vocational qualifications*, McIntosh, CEE, 2004.

[20] *Alternative skills scenarios to 2020 for the UK economy: Report to the Leitch Review of Skills*, HM Treasury/SSDA, CE/IER, 2005.

[21] *We can work it out: the impact of technological change on the demand for low-skill workers*, Manning, CEP Discussion Paper 640, 2004; *Lousy and lovely jobs: the rising polarisation of work in Britain*, Goos and Manning, 2003.

Flexibility and security 1.28   As global economic change continues, people's economic security will be ensured in different ways to the past. In the past, attempts to ensure people's economic security often focused on trying to protect particular jobs. In the new global economy, it is simply not possible to hold back the tide of change in this way. Instead, people's economic security is best delivered by ensuring their flexibility. Skills are one of the best ways to deliver flexibility, allowing people to adapt to change and retrain, reducing the risk that they become cut off from labour market opportunity.

The changing UK workforce

1.29   At the same time as the global economy restructures, significant changes are taking place in the UK workforce and the pool of labour that UK firms can draw on. The UK population is ageing and global migration flows are increasing, widening the pool of labour businesses can draw from. Many older workers will have to reskill as the UK economy restructures in response to global changes and working lives lengthen.

Demographic change 1.30   These changes have important implications for the UK economy. Over 70 per cent of the 2020 working age population are already over the age of 16. In the past, structural change was facilitated by a flow into expanding industries of young people with more relevant skills and the flow out of declining industries by older people leaving the workforce. A strengthening flow of skilled young people is essential for improving the UK's prosperity. However, as the population ages and working lives lengthen, adult workers are more likely to have to update their skills to move into new sectors or adapt to new technologies.

Migration 1.31   Global migration flows have been increasing over the past 30 years. Net migration to the UK was 185,000 in 2005. The expansion of the EU has added to the pool of labour from which UK firms can draw their workforce. The latest estimates show that around 510,000 people from the A8 accession countries have registered to work in the UK between May 2004 and September 2006, but this does not indicate the number of long-term migrants into the UK since most come for only short periods and many may have either returned home or plan to do so.[22] Migration generally has a positive effect, helping to mitigate skills shortages and fill jobs that cannot be filled domestically. A recent study found no evidence that migration impacts on the employment, economic activity, unemployment or wages of the resident population.[23] The increased flow of immigration from the accession countries has had little or no impact on the wages or claimant unemployment of any group of domestic workers.[24] However, the perception is that individual competition for jobs increases in the short-term.

1.32   The Government is introducing a new system for migrants from outside the EU, awarding points to those applying on the basis of their characteristics such as skill level.[25] This aims to ensure that future migration from outside the EU is focused on those with high skills and filling skills gaps and shortages. Net migration is extremely difficult to accurately predict. However, official Government projections are for net migration of around 145,000 each year from 2007 onwards, over 90 per cent of which are of working age. This accounts for around two thirds of the growth in the working age population between now and 2020.[26]

---

[22] *Accession monitoring report May 2004 – September 2006*, Home Office, DWP, HMRC and DCLG, 2006. The A8 countries are: Czech Republic, Estonia, Hungary, Latvia, Lithuania, Poland, Slovakia and Slovenia.

[23] *The impact of immigration on the UK labour market*, Dustmann, Fabbri and Preston, 2005.

[24] *The impact of free movement of workers from Central and Eastern Europe on the UK labour market*, DWP, 2006.

[25] *A points based system: Making migration work for Britain*, Home Office Command Paper, 2006.

[26] GAD population projections, 2004.

SKILLS AND FAIRNESS

1.33   Skills are a key driver of fairness, ensuring that everyone can share in the benefits of growth, reducing inequalities and helping ensure no group, region or area is left behind. The transformation taking place in the global economy makes this role even more important. Without greater equality of access to skills improvements, disparities will increase further.

Disparities between areas

1.34   Output and employment have increased in all regions and countries of the UK, but disparities between regions and countries remain high, and disparities between local areas are significantly larger than the European average. The gap in prosperity between parts of the UK is greater than the gap between the UK and the USA – Gross Domestic Product (GDP) per head in London is more than double that in Liverpool.[27]

1.35   The different skills mixes of each region and country of the UK partly explain these persistent disparities. These skills mixes differ for a number of reasons, including the lower attainment of qualifications by young people in some areas and the fact that some of those that do gain higher qualifications in some regions move to the south of England, where many high skill jobs are currently to be found.

Income inequality

1.36   In addition to significant disparities in regional living standards, income inequality is high in the UK. Income inequality in the UK rose substantially during the 1980s and early 1990s. In 1976, the richest 10 per cent earned 2.9 times the poorest 10 per cent. Twenty five years later they were earning four times as much as the poorest. Though the level of income inequality has stabilised since then, it remains high both by historic and international standards.

1.37   This rise in overall income inequality was associated with a rise in relative child poverty.[28] By 1997, the UK had, at 25 per cent, the highest rate of child poverty in the EU. The incidence of child poverty has fallen over the past decade, but remains among the highest in Europe, as shown in Chart 1.3.

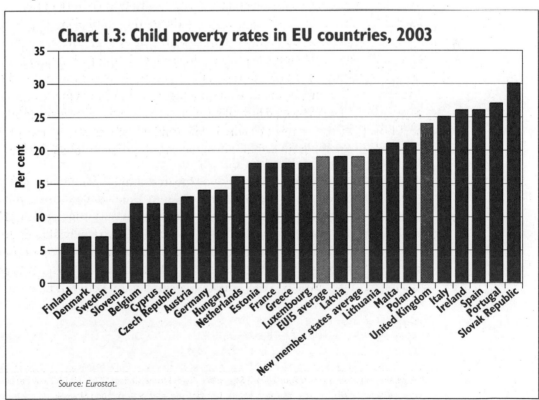

Chart 1.3: Child poverty rates in EU countries, 2003

Source: Eurostat.

---

[27] Barclays Bank, 2001 in *Urban renaissance of EU non-capital cities*, Parkinson et al, 2004.

[28] Child poverty can be measured in a number of ways. The most common, and the one used by the Government, is the proportion of children living in households with less than 60 per cent of median income.

1.38 A wide range of factors influences the income distribution and the number of children in relative low-income poverty. Many of these factors have contributed to the rise in inequality seen up until the mid 1990s. Skills and qualifications are a key determinant of income. Consequently, the relatively polarised distribution of qualifications in the UK would lead to a wide distribution of earnings. This impact was reinforced by changes taking place in the global economy over this period, which, as discussed above, have increased the wage premium for skilled workers.[29] By raising the incomes of low earning parents, skills improvements help lift children out of poverty.

Life chances **1.39** As well as reducing income inequality, improvements in skills can improve people's life chances, giving them the opportunity to progress and move into higher paid jobs. Social mobility is low in the UK – there is significant correlation between parents' position in the earnings distribution and the position their children achieve. Estimates vary but suggest that a significant proportion of a child's income, maybe more than one quarter, can be explained by the income of their parents.[30] This correlation is higher in the UK than in many other countries and has risen in the post-war period, again in contrast to falls in other countries.[31]

1.40 In the UK, the links between educational attainment and family background are strong. Children with parents from unskilled manual backgrounds, and whose parents tend to have fewer qualifications, have a 20 per cent probability of achieving five or more GCSEs at grade A*-C, compared with 69 per cent for children with managerial or professional parents.[32] Furthermore, the link between family income and the probability of entering higher education has strengthened in recent years.[33]

1.41 Education is closely related to income. The strong, persistent and, in some cases, strengthening links between family background and educational attainment are likely to be a significant part of the reason that social mobility is low in the UK by international standards and has fallen in recent decades. Evidence suggests that greater equality of opportunity in education is a key driver of the higher social mobility seen in countries such as Canada.[34]

Wider social **1.42** There are important links between skills and wider social outcomes, such as health,
impacts crime and social cohesion. Skills also have important impacts on financial capability, helping households to manage the family finances, and family life, allowing parents to help their children with their homework.[35]

1.43 Health problems, including depression and obesity, are more common in unskilled and low-income households. Skills can impact on health either directly, by providing information on improving health, or indirectly, by improving income and making a healthy lifestyle more affordable. It is difficult to estimate the potential health benefits of skills improvements, but they are likely to be greatest at the bottom end of the skills distribution. One study suggests that moving 50 per cent of women currently without qualifications to Level 1 would have benefits of between £300 million and £1.9 billion per annum in terms of reduced obesity and depression.[36]

[29] For a summary of the literature see, *The assessment: globalisation and labour market adjustment*, Greenaway and Nelson, Oxford Review of Economic Policy, Volume 16, Number 3, 2000.

[30] *Family income and educational attainment: A review of approaches and evidence for Britain*, Blanden and Gregg, Oxford Review of Economic Policy, 2, 245-263, 2004.

[31] *Intergenerational mobility in Europe and North America*, Blanden, Gregg and Machin, CEP, LSE, 2005.

[32] *Education and skills: The economic benefit*, DfES, 2003.

[33] *Higher education, family income and changes in intergenerational mobility*, Machin in *The labour market under New Labour: The state of working Britain*, Dickens, Gregg and Wadsworth (eds), 2003.

[34] *Generational Income Mobility in North America and Europe*, Corak (ed), 2004, Cambridge University Press; *Intergenerational Mobility in Europe and North America*, Blanden, Gregg and Machin, 2005.

[35] *Education and skills: The economic benefit*, DfES, 2003.

[36] *Quantitative estimates of the social benefits of learning, 2: Health (depression and obesity)*, Centre for Research on the Wider Benefits of Learning, Feinstein, 2002.

1.44   Those on lower incomes are both more likely to be victims of crime and more likely to commit crime. Offenders are far less likely to have qualifications and so tend to have poorer pay and employment prospects: more than one half of offenders have no qualifications, compared to 15 per cent of the population as a whole.[37] Skills can affect crime by improving an individual's employment, pay and progression and hence increasing the opportunity cost of offending, and by reducing income inequality.[38] While it is extremely difficult to quantify the impact of skills on crime, one study found that the benefits from reduced crime of a 1 percentage point increase in the proportion of the working age population with GCSE or equivalent qualifications could be £10-320 million per annum.[39]

1.45   This chapter has set out the increasing importance of skills to prosperity and fairness. The next chapter sets out the Review's analysis of the UK's skills base and the balance of responsibility between government, employers and individuals for delivering it.

CONCLUSION

1.46   This Review was established to consider the UK's optimal skills mix in order to maximise growth, productivity and fairness by 2020. Skills are increasingly critical for the UK to meet the long-term challenge of increasing prosperity through higher productivity and employment at a time when the global economy is changing rapidly. These global changes are increasing the number of high skilled jobs and increasing skills demands within most existing jobs. Increasingly, no one is immune from the increased demand for skills. Skills are also increasingly critical if the UK is to become a fairer society, reducing inequality and poverty and ensuring everyone has a fair chance in life.

1.47   The Review has concluded that it is critical for the future health of the economy and society that the UK be a world leader in skills. The next chapter sets out how the UK's skills base stacks up against this requirement and the changing balance of responsibility between employers, individuals and government for driving improvements in the UK's skills base.

---

[37] *Skills: getting on in business, getting on at work*, DfES White Paper, 2005.

[38] *Crime and economic incentives*, Machin and Meghir, Institute for Fiscal Studies, 2000.

[39] *Quantitative estimates of the social benefits of learning, 1: Crime*, Feinstein, Centre for Research on the Wider Benefits of Leaning, 2002.

2 THE UK'S SKILLS BASE

Chapter summary

The previous chapter set out how global economic changes are decisively increasing the importance of skills to UK prosperity and fairness. This chapter sets out how the UK's skills base matches up to the challenge of global change and how the responsibility for improving skills has been shared.

The UK's skills base has suffered from deficits built up over a long period of time as a result of historic failings in the education and training systems. It has improved significantly over recent years as reforms have begun to succeed in driving improvements. The proportion of adults with high skills has risen from 21 per cent in 1994 to 29 per cent in 2005 and the proportion with no qualifications has fallen from 22 per cent to 13 per cent. Despite this, the UK's skills base remains mediocre by international standards. 7 million adults lack functional numeracy and 5 million lack functional literacy. The proportion of adults aged 25 to 64 with low or no qualifications is more than double that in Sweden, Japan and Canada. The proportion of adults with high skills is internationally comparable, but not world leading.

The Government and Devolved Administrations have already set stretching targets to improve the skills of young people and adults, which will be challenging to achieve. The Review's analysis shows that meeting these would drive significant improvements. Other countries are improving their skills bases too and so the UK is projected to remain no better than average in skills, running to stand still. This will have profound implications for the UK as the global economy changes, holding back prosperity, constraining businesses' ability to compete and preventing people from succeeding in the labour market. There is a clear and pressing need for the UK to go further and commit to being a world leader in skills.

The Government, employers and individuals all invest in skills improvements. The balance of responsibilities has changed over time and varied between centralised and local approaches, often supply-driven and switching between voluntarism and compulsion. Previous approaches have relied on planning to meet collectively articulated skills needs. This has constrained employer and individual engagement. The framework today is based on voluntary action, with employers in a sector able to act collectively. There are encouraging signs that the current system is beginning to deliver results, with the Government working in partnership with employers by delivering flexible training through the popular Train to Gain service in England, employers articulating their needs through Sector Skills Councils and a significant increase in attainment of skills by young people and adults.

The Review has concluded that the UK needs to build on recent, encouraging progress if the UK is to meet the global challenge ahead and be a world leader in skills. The next chapter sets out the Review's recommendations for a national commitment to world class skills and a new partnership to achieve it.

2.1   The previous chapter set out the Review's analysis of the critical importance of skills to the UK economy. It set out how global economic changes are decisively increasing the importance of skills to prosperity, employment and social justice. This chapter sets out the UK's current skills base, the way in which it is delivered and how the UK needs to go further and faster if it is to achieve the world class skills base it needs to succeed in the new global economy.

CHANGES IN THE UK'S SKILLS BASE

2.2   The UK's skills base has been historically weak, the product of longstanding failures in the education and training system. Over recent years, the UK's skills base has improved significantly, with rising standards at schools and colleges, significantly more young people going to university and improvements in the skills of adults. Despite this, the Review has found that the UK's skills base remains mediocre by international standards.

The UK's current skills mix

2.3   The UK's skills base suffers from longstanding historic failures in the education and training system. In recent years, it has improved significantly. The number of working age people in England qualified to Level 2 is estimated to have risen by over 1 million since 2003. The proportion of adults with a high qualification has risen from 21 per cent in 1994 to 29 per cent in 2005. The proportion of people with no qualifications has nearly halved, down from 21 per cent to 13 per cent. There is further to go to fully tackle the UK's historic weaknesses in skills. Chart 2.1 shows how the UK's adult population (25 to state pension age) compares to other countries in the Organisation for Economic Co-operation and Development (OECD).

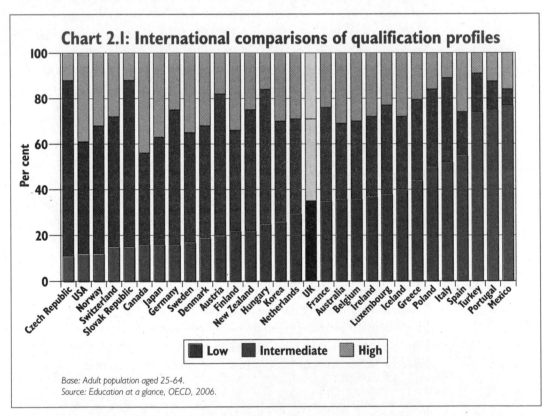

Chart 2.1: International comparisons of qualification profiles

Base: Adult population aged 25-64.
Source: Education at a glance, OECD, 2006.

2.4   Other countries have invested in their skills over the long-term and so the UK is ranked:

- 17th out of the 30 OECD countries in the proportion who have low or no qualifications (equivalent to less than a Level 2 in the UK), with 35 per cent at this level, more than double the proportion in the best performing nations, such as the USA, Canada, Germany and Sweden;

- 20th in the proportion with intermediate qualifications (Levels 2 and 3) with 36 per cent qualified to this level, compared to more than 50 per cent in Germany and New Zealand; and

- 11th in the proportion who have high qualifications (Level 4 and above), with 29 per cent qualified to this level, internationally comparable but still well behind the USA, Japan and Canada where the proportion stands at around 40 per cent.

2.5   The UK's significant deficits at low and intermediate skill levels have been widely acknowledged. Although the proportion of adults aged 25 to 64 lacking Level 2 qualifications (according to OECD definitions) has fallen by around one quarter between 1998 and 2004, the proportion of adults in the UK lacking at least a Level 2 qualification is more than double that of the best performing countries. More than 50 per cent of adults in countries such as Germany and Norway are qualified to intermediate level, compared to fewer than 40 per cent in the UK.

2.6   The UK is internationally comparable at the top end as a result of recent progress, but not world leading. The proportion of adults aged 25 to 64 qualified at a high level of qualification (according to OECD definitions – broadly equating to Level 4 or above) was 29 per cent in 2004. In countries such as the USA, Japan and Canada, around 40 per cent of the adult population is qualified to high level.

2.7   The skills profile varies across the different regions and countries in the UK. For example, Scotland has both a higher proportion of its working age population (31 per cent) with at least a Level 4 qualification compared with the UK average, and a smaller proportion (28 per cent) with less than a Level 2 qualification. Wales and Northern Ireland have 34 and 35 per cent respectively of their adult populations without a Level 2 and 24 and 23 per cent respectively qualified at Level 4 or above.

Impact on business   **2.8**   It is difficult to measure the impact of skills deficits on public and private employers. There is considerable debate over the accuracy of reported skills deficiencies, how persistent they are and the significance of their impact on performance and productivity. Employers in England reported 571,000 vacancies at the time of the National Employer Skills Survey 2005 (NESS), of which one in four were hard to fill because of a lack of suitably skilled applicants. They reported a further 1.3 million employees as not fully proficient at their job.[1] There were similar findings in Scotland.[2]

2.9   Employers in the survey felt that soft skills were lacking (particularly team working and customer handling skills, each of which were mentioned as lacking in one half of all workers lacking proficiency). Technical, practical or job-specific skills were seen to be lacking in over two fifths of employees with a skills gap. Other generic, soft skills such as oral communication, problem-solving and written communication skills were the next most commonly reported skills gaps. A lack of literacy and numeracy skills were each present in one fifth of reported skill gaps. The Confederation of British Industry's (CBI) recent Employer Trends Survey found that employers place the highest priority for training on leadership and management skills.[3] Chart 2.2 shows the spread of skills gaps across occupations.

---

[1] *National Employer Skills Survey*, Learning and Skills Council, 2005.

[2] *Skills in Scotland*, Futureskills Scotland, 2004.

[3] *Employer Trends Survey*, CBI, 2006.

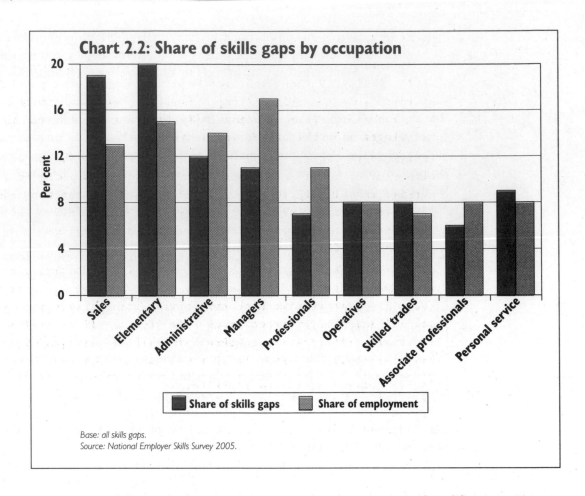

Chart 2.2: Share of skills gaps by occupation

Legend: ■ Share of skills gaps   ▨ Share of employment

Base: all skills gaps.
Source: National Employer Skills Survey 2005.

Basic skills **2.10**   Some skills can be measured directly, rather than in terms of qualifications. Literacy and numeracy skills, for example, can be tested irrespective of the qualifications a person holds. In 1996, the International Adult Literacy Survey (IALS) found that Britain had the 10th highest proportion of people lacking functional literacy of the 12 countries that took part.[4] Box 2.1 summarises the UK's performance in basic skills.

---

[4] *Adult Literacy in Britain*, Carey, Low and Hansbro, ONS, 1997.

Box 2.1: Measuring basic skills

The UK uses five levels to measure literacy and numeracy skills: Entry Levels 1, 2 and 3, Level 1 and Level 2. The Moser Report identified Level 1 literacy and Entry Level 3 numeracy as the standards necessary to function at work and society in general.[a] An example of an Entry Level 3 numeracy skill is being able to add or subtract money using decimal notation, or being able to work with fractions.

Surveys, like the Skills for Life Survey conducted in 2003, assess people's basic skill levels using a variety of literacy and numeracy problems corresponding to the five levels described above. In 2003, 16 per cent of the working age population in England, over five million people, lacked Level 1 literacy skills and 21 per cent (6.8 million) lacked Entry Level 3 numeracy skills. More than 15 million people in England lacked Level 1 numeracy skills, equivalent to a GCSE Maths at grades D–G.

International surveys, such as the OECD's International Adult Literacy Survey and the more recent Adult Literacy and Life Skills Survey, use similar techniques to the Skills for Life Survey. They show that, while many other countries have a large number of adults with low basic skills, the UK lies in the bottom half of the OECD. Sweden had the lowest proportion of adults who had less than the equivalent of UK Level 1 literacy at just 7.5 per cent in 1994, (compared with 21.8 per cent in the UK in 1996) and just 5 per cent of 26 to 35 year-olds.

[a] A fresh start: Improving literacy and numeracy, DfEE, 1999.

2.11   Despite recent policy initiatives, the UK retains a large and significant basic skills problem.[5] Chart 2.3 shows the distribution of literacy and numeracy skills in 2003. Analysis of the best available evidence suggests that in the UK around 6 million working age people lacked functional literacy skills and nearly 8 million lacked functional numeracy skills in 2003. The Government, as part of its basic skills strategy Skills for Life, has delivered over 1.25 million Skills for Life qualifications since 2001, exceeding its 2005 target of 1 million achievements. By 2006, 5 million lacked functional literacy and 7 million lacked functional numeracy.

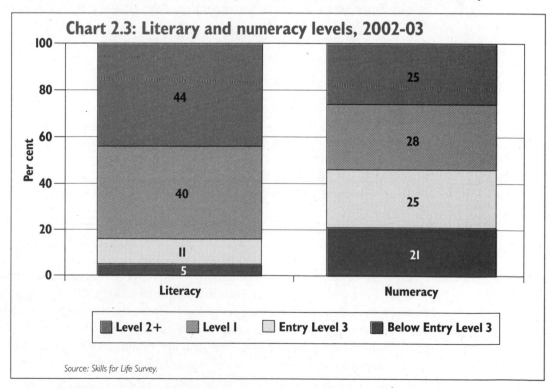
Chart 2.3: Literary and numeracy levels, 2002-03
Source: Skills for Life Survey.

[5] The Skills for Life Survey – A national needs and impact survey of literacy, numeracy and ICT skills, DfES, 2003; National Survey of Adult Basic Skills in Wales, 2004.

The UK's future skills mix

Qualification profile 2.12 The Government and the Devolved Administrations have set stretching targets to continue the improvements in the UK's skills base seen over the past decade. Table 2.1 sets out the main targets to improve skills among both young people and adults across the UK.

Table 2.1: Key UK targets to improve skills

England

By 2008, 60 per cent of those aged 16 to achieve the equivalent of 5 GCSEs at grades A–C.

Increase the proportion of 19-year olds who achieve at least Level 2 by 3 percentage points between 2004 and 2006, and a further 2 percentage points between 2006 and 2008.

Improve the basic skills of 2.25 million adults between the launch of Skills for Life in 2001 and 2010, with a milestone of 1.5 million in 2007.

Reducing by at least 40 per cent the number of adults in the workforce who lack NVQ2 or equivalent qualifications by 2010, with a milestone of 1.5 million in 2007.

Reducing by at least 40 per cent the number of adults in the workforce who lack NVQ2 or equivalent qualifications by 2010. Working towards this, 1 million adults in the workforce to achieve Level 2 between 2003 and 2006.

By 2010, increase participation in higher education towards 50 per cent of those aged 18 to 30.

Scotland

The Scottish Executive does not have PSA targets. Instead, they have a series of high level indicators contained within their Lifelong Learning Strategy. The suite of indicators focus on similar areas of skill as the PSAs for the rest of the UK.[a]

Northern Ireland

By 2007, 63 per cent of year 12 pupils to obtain 5 or more GCSEs (or equivalent) at grades A–C (or equivalent), compared with 59 per cent in 2002.

By 2007, 97 per cent of year 14 pupils to obtain 2+ A levels at grades A–E, compared with 95 per cent in 2002.

To increase the proportion of working age people qualified at Level 2 or above from 63 per cent in summer 2003 to 68 per cent in spring 2007.

To increase the proportion of working age people qualified at Level 3 or above from 46 per cent in summer 2003 to 48 per cent in spring 2007.

By 2007, 18,500 people will have achieved a recognised qualification in Essential Skills compared with 100 in March 2003.

Wales

By 2010, over three quarters of pupils finish compulsory education attaining at least 5 GCSEs at grades A*–C or equivalent.

By 2010, reduce the proportion of adults of working age without qualifications from 1 in 4 in 1996 to 1 in 10. By 2010, increase the proportion of adults of working age with a Level 4 qualification from 1 in 5 in 1996 to over 3 in 10.

[a]The lifelong learning strategy for Scotland, Scottish Executive, 2003.

2.13 These targets will be challenging to achieve. In particular, it will be very challenging to meet the target to reduce the number of adults lacking a Level 2 qualification in England by 2010. Participation by young people in higher education has remained at around 43 per cent in recent years, leading some people to challenge the attainability of a 50 per cent participation rate. If all targets are met and are combined with improvements brought about as increasingly well-qualified young people flow into the adult population, the UK's qualification profile will improve significantly by 2020. Chart 2.4 sets out projections for the UK's adult population.

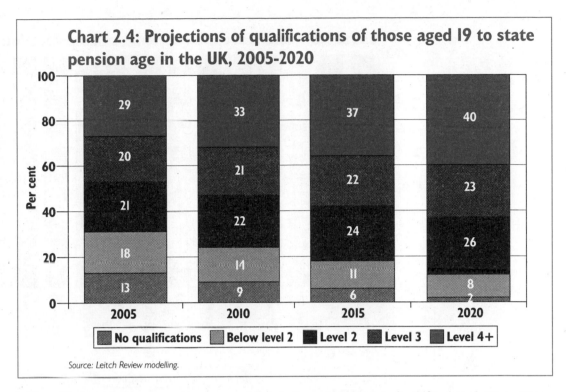

Chart 2.4: Projections of qualifications of those aged 19 to state pension age in the UK, 2005-2020

Source: Leitch Review modelling.

2.14   If these improvements were achieved, the proportion of adults (aged 19 to State Pension age) without any formal qualifications would fall from 13 per cent (4.6 million) in 2005 to 2 per cent (0.6 million) in 2020. The proportion with high qualifications would rise from 29 per cent (10.1 million) in 2005 to 40 per cent (15.6 million) by 2020. Despite this, significant weaknesses would remain. Around 3.9 million adults would lack the equivalent of a basic school leaving qualification.

International comparisons   **2.15**   Other countries are also improving their skills profile. While it is hard to be accurate about their probable position in 2020, the Review has produced projections, shown in Chart 2.5. All OECD projections are based on the population aged 25 to 64, so the UK figures in Chart 2.5 differ slightly from those in Chart 2.4, which is based on the adult population, those aged 19 to 64. Further details on the methodology used in these projections can be found in the Leitch Review Interim Report.

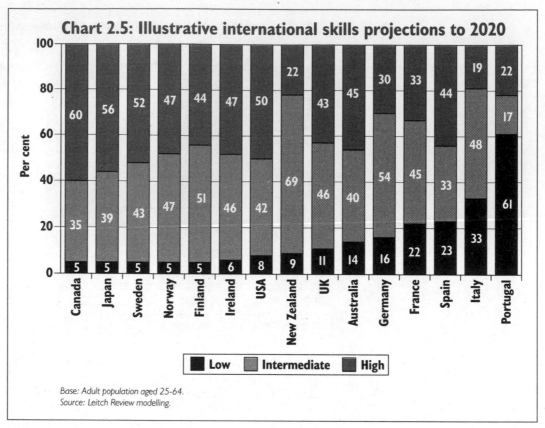

Chart 2.5: Illustrative international skills projections to 2020

Base: Adult population aged 25-64.
Source: Leitch Review modelling.

2.16 Chart 2.5 shows that the UK's relative position could improve if challenging projections were met, but would remain far from world class:

- gaining two places to 15th out of 30 in low skills, with 11 per cent of those aged over 25 still lacking the equivalent of a basic school leaving qualification, more than double that of the best performing OECD countries;

- rising seven places to 13th in intermediate skills, with 46 per cent of those aged over 25 qualified to this level, but still far below the levels in Germany, New Zealand and Finland among others; and

- 13th in terms of those aged over 25 who have attained high qualifications, with 43 per cent compared to more than 50 per cent in the USA, Canada, Sweden and Japan.

2.17 The Review's analysis shows that by 2020 the UK could move up the international league table if challenging projections were met, but would still remain average by OECD standards. It will remain mediocre for low level skills with more than double the proportion of people lacking a basic platform of skills than the best performing countries. It will rise in intermediate skills, but only on a definition that includes Level 2 and only to 13th out of the 30 OECD countries. Despite the substantial increase in the proportion of people qualified to Level 4 or above, the UK will be 13th in high skills. The UK is on track to achieve the same proportion of high skill workers that the US and Canada have today.

Literacy and **2.18** The Review has also looked at how the UK's basic skills profile is likely to change by **numeracy** 2020. The proportion of the working age population lacking basic literacy or numeracy is likely to fall. This will be a result of achieving current targets, planned improvements to GCSEs and the effect of younger people replacing less-skilled, older people in the working age population.[6] However, the UK's basic skills problem is unlikely to even be halved. Chart 2.6

---

[6] Box 3.3 in the Interim Report explains the modelling process the Review has used to generate projections to 2020.

shows that around 4 million adults will still lack functional literacy skills at Level 1, 1.3 million less than today. More than 6 million people will lack functional numeracy skills, 0.9 million less than today.

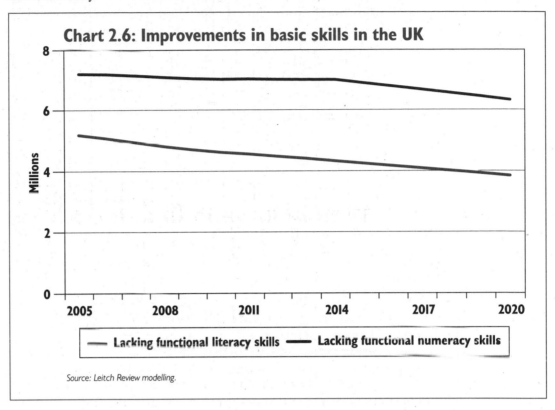

Chart 2.6: Improvements in basic skills in the UK

Source: Leitch Review modelling.

2.19   As with formal qualifications, it is very difficult to project the basic skills profiles of other countries. International surveys are rare and trends cannot be extrapolated to 2020. The largest international survey, IALS, provides some useful insights. The basic skills profile that the UK is on track to achieve by 2020 would not even be world class in today's terms. In 1994, when the OECD IALS survey was conducted, just 7.5 per cent of the working age population in Sweden lacked functional literacy, compared with the projected 10 per cent for the UK in 2020. Other countries are improving fast. Just 5 per cent of those aged 26 to 35 in Sweden lacked functional literacy skills. Without greater ambition it is clear that the UK is far from on track to have world class basic skills by 2020.

DELIVERING SKILLS IN THE UK

2.20   The challenge of delivering economically valuable skills has been a longstanding concern for the UK. Even back in 1776, Adam Smith's *'The Wealth of Nations'* suggested that *'the greater part of what is taught in schools and universities ... does not seem to be the proper preparation for that of business'.*

A brief history **2.21**   The responsibility for delivering improvements in skills has always been shared **of skills** between government, employers and individuals. The balance of responsibilities between the three has changed over time and has varied between centralised and local approaches, often supply-driven and switching between voluntarism and compulsion. Throughout, action to improve the skills of adults has aimed to engage employers, increasing their investment in skills and articulating their needs to ensure that the skills delivered are economically valuable.

2.22   Action to increase employer investment in skills has varied between compelling employers to invest in skills and encouraging voluntary action. In 1964, a period of compulsory training activity for employers began with the introduction of Industrial Training Boards (ITBs) and a training levy system. In 1973, the Manpower Services Commission (MSC) was established to plan workforce skill needs, also with statutory powers to improve skills and training amongst employers.

2.23   By the 1980s, most of the Industrial Training Boards were abolished and more voluntarist initiatives and organisations introduced to replace them. In their place Training and Enterprise Councils (TECs) were launched in 1989, as employer-led bodies to assess local training needs, fund and encourage employer investment in training.

2.24   In 1990, Investors in People was established as a voluntary system to encourage employers to invest in skills. By 1992, the Further and Higher Education Act saw the creation of the Further Education Funding Council (FEFC), the Office for Standards in Education (OfSTED), the removal of further education (FE) colleges from Local Authority control and the granting of university status to the UK's polytechnics.

2.25   In 2001, the FEFC and the TECs ended and the Learning and Skills Council (LSC) was created in their place. The LSC would plan, fund and secure the provision of post-16 education and training in England (excluding higher education) to help improve England's skills profile. In 2001, National Training Organisations (NTOs) were replaced by the Skills for Business Network comprising Sector Skills Councils (SSCs) and the Sector Skills Development Agency (SSDA). Sector Skills Councils, through Sector Skills Agreements, were to engage employers in the design of qualifications and training as well as identifying and working to tackle skills shortages and gaps.

2.26   There have been a number of efforts to enable employers to articulate their skills needs so that the skills system can deliver economically valuable skills. These have often been integrated with approaches to raise employer investment. For example, the MSC carried out manpower planning and had statutory powers to compel employers to increase training to meet these. The NTOs and TECs could not compel employers to train but were responsible for assessing needs at sector and local levels and these assessments were used in planning publicly funded provision.

2.27   The previous system was focused on asking employers to collectively articulate their future skills needs and then trying to plan to meet these needs. Too often, collective articulation of future skills needs has been an ineffective and inefficient mechanism. As a result, too much provision has been supply driven, based on trying to predict and provide. Consequently, employers were reluctant to contribute toward training costs because they did not have confidence in the quality of training on offer and felt frustrated by the lack of influence over qualifications. At the same time, they felt let down by poor levels of basic literacy and numeracy resulting from a failing school system.

2.28   People were unable to access quality training at a time and place that fitted in with their job, had little choice over training and faced a complex system of financial support. The Government saw its role as protecting people from change through income support, rather than preparing them for it through skills support. It focused on overseeing a training system that tried to predict and provide future skill needs from the centre, rather than empowering people and employers to make the right training decisions for themselves.

2.29 The impact of this was seen in:

- too little investment by employers in their workers;

- too little responsibility taken by individuals for their own learning;

- a qualification system divorced from the needs of the modern workplace; and

- a welfare system that did not meet the needs of a fast changing economy.

Current balance of responsibilities

2.30 Over the last decade, the division of responsibilities for improving adult skills between government, employers and individuals has evolved further. The Government has taken steps to build a more flexible, demand-led skills system. A major recent innovation in England has been Train to Gain, which offers employers support in designing and sourcing flexibly delivered training to meet their needs, with government funds to pay the full cost of training for eligible employers up to Level 2 and support for wider training beyond that level. The Employer Training Pilots, on which the rollout of Train to Gain is based, proved successful at engaging employers and employees and are popular with business: 30,000 employers and 250,000 employees had participated by March 2006.

2.31 There are encouraging signs that the current system of SSCs is bedding down well, with some examples of excellence. In 2005, 62 per cent of employers who had engaged with their SSC in the last year rated their satisfaction at six out of ten or better.[7] Employers, through SSCs, can introduce measures, such as levies and licences to practise, where a clear majority in that sector support it.

Box 2.2: A demand-led system

The Review's analysis shows that previous approaches to delivering skills have been too 'supply driven', based on the Government asking employers to articulate their needs and then planning supply to meet this. This approach has a poor track record. Employers are confused by the plethora of advisory, strategic and planning bodies they are asked to input to. Under a planned system, the incentives are for providers to continue doing what they have done in the past so long as it meets the planning requirements, rather than responding flexibly as demand changes. As a result, less than 10 per cent of employer training is in FE.

Recent reforms have attempted to develop a more 'demand led' system, responding to demand rather than trying to plan supply. Train to Gain provides flexible training, designed to meet the needs of employers and employees. Providers only receive funding if they effectively meet the needs of their customers. The Employer Training Pilots show that this approach leads to provision that better reflects the needs of consumers increasing relevance, completion rates and therefore value for money.

The Review has concluded that this sort of approach must be embedded across the system so that providers only receive funding as they attract customers, rather than receiving a block grant and planning provision to meet expected demand. Building a demand-led system is the only way in which to increase employer and individual investment in skills and ensure that increased investment delivers economically valuable skills.

---

[7] Sector Skills Development Agency, 2006.

2.32   There have been other areas of significant progress. The number of Apprentices in learning has grown from 76,000 in 1997 to 256,000 in 2005.[8] Today around 42 per cent of young people participate in higher education and the proportion of adults with a degree level qualification has risen to 29 per cent. The Government has exceeded its target of 750,000 adults taking basic skills qualifications in 2004 and is well on the way to meeting the 2010 target of 2.25 million adults improving their basic skills. Latest data suggests that the Government has also met the interim 2006 target of one million additional adults gaining full Level 2 qualifications in England.

Current investment in skills

2.33   Employers, individuals and the Government all invest significantly in skills improvements. In England employers spend around £2.4 billion on direct course costs and up to £17.4 billion in total, excluding the wages of employees.[9] Employer investment in skills varies significantly by type of employee, type of employer and sector of the economy. Training by employers is disproportionately focused on highly-skilled workers, who are five times more likely to be trained at work than low skill workers.[10] Around one third of firms do no training at all, and this varies between 50 per cent of employers in some sectors to just under 5 per cent in the best performing sectors.

2.34   The Government in England invests around £12 billion on adult skills each year, of which around £4.5 billion is on further education (FE), including work-based learning, and £7.4 billion on higher education (HE). These are the overall costs of tuition, learner support and capital. Individuals will pay £1.35 billion per annum through the new variable tuition fees, on top of the existing £0.9 billion per annum income from standard fees.

2.35   However, the combined level of investment compares poorly by international standards. Although the overall proportion of adults trained is relatively high (61 per cent), only 19 per cent of adults in the UK report contributing any of their own funding towards education and training, compared with an OECD average of 37 per cent.[11] In addition funding for higher education in the UK from both public and private sources is low by international standards – less than one half that in the USA and 40 per cent lower than in Sweden.[12]

Employer investment in training

2.36   Employers can improve the skills of their employees in a number of ways: through 'in-house' training, private training providers and the publicly funded system. Businesses are best placed to make a judgement about which is the most appropriate channel for them. The Government must ensure that the publicly funded system meets the needs of individuals and employers. Following on from training, employers need to use improved skills effectively in order to derive a return from their investment and for people to gain from higher wages.

2.37   Much employer investment in skills takes place outside the publicly funded system. More than one half of this is spent on on-the-job training and the wages of employees when in training.[13] 12 per cent of employees receive training to nationally recognised qualifications each year, and 6 per cent receive training in NVQs. Less than 10 per cent of employer training is delivered by FE providers. Chart 2.8 shows a breakdown of employer investment in training.

2.38   On the job training is a vital source of skills development and not all training should be formal. However, focusing as much training as possible on qualifications, as long as qualifications reflect economically valuable skills, brings enormous benefits to both individuals and employers. Employers are prepared to pay significantly higher wages for

[8] *Departmental Report*, DfES, 2006.

[9] *National employer skills survey*, LSC, 2005

[10] *Labour Force Survey*, Spring 2006.

[11] See *Adults in training: an international comparison of continuing education training*, O'Connell, Economic and Social Research Institute/OECD, 1999.

[12] *Education at a glance*, OECD, 2006.

[13] *National Employer Skills Survey*, Learning and Skills Council, 2006.

those with qualifications. For example, the return to a degree is estimated at around 25 per cent and the returns to GCSEs are around 25 per cent.[14]

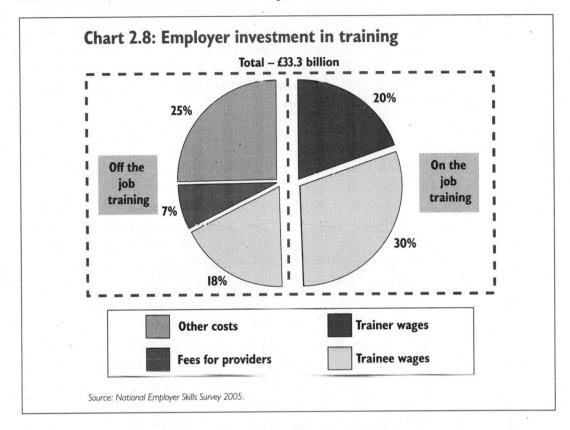

Chart 2.8: Employer investment in training

Total – £33.3 billion

Off the job training: 25%, 7%

On the job training: 20%, 30%, 18%

Legend: Other costs | Trainer wages | Fees for providers | Trainee wages

Source: National Employer Skills Survey 2005.

2.39   For individuals, they provide portability in the labour market, allowing them to demonstrate the skills they have acquired. For employers, they provide valuable signals when recruiting new workers and also motivate employees to complete their training. Qualifications form a major part of employer recruitment strategies, especially screening candidates prior to shortlisting or interview.[15] As a result, both individuals and employers value qualifications. The majority of individuals prefer studying towards a qualification,[16] and over one half of employers feel it is quite or very important that the training provided led to a qualification.[17]

Skills and employment   **2.40**   The Review has found that the skills and employment systems, which should work in tandem to improve people's chances, are disjointed. Welfare to Work focuses on people's short-term prospects, but not long-term help. There are no effective links between someone moving into work from the New Deal and in work support, such as Train to Gain in England, that can help them stay in work and progress. People face many fragmented sources of support that provide help in organisational 'silos' rather than focusing on helping the individual to 'get on in life'. As a result, individuals do not receive the support they need and are unsure how and where to access it. Chapter 7 has more details.

[14] See, for example, *Returns to education: A non-technical summary of CEE work and policy discussion*, Sianesi, Institute for Fiscal Studies and Centre for the Economics of Education, 2003.
[15] *Recruitment, Retention and Turnover Survey*, CIPD, 2006.
[16] *National Adult Learning Survey*, National Centre for Social Research, DfES, Research Report 415, 2002.
[17] *The Market for Qualifications in the UK*, PWC, 2005.

Effective use of skills

2.41   Skills are a derived demand: employers' skills needs are a consequence both of their product strategy and the firm's characteristics. Management is a key determinant of an employer's product or service strategy and whether skills are used effectively. The quality of management and leadership varies both between and within sectors. Comparative research on a wide range of best management practices in manufacturing firms in the USA, UK, France and Germany has shown USA firms to be the best managed and UK firms to be the most poorly managed.[18] In addition, a low proportion of employers in the UK with managerial staff provide training for them.[19]

Meeting the global challenge

2.42   The Review has found that the UK is tackling its historic skills deficit. It is on track to deliver further significant skills improvements by 2020. These are driven by promising advances in building a demand led system and engaging employers. However, other countries are improving their skills too, often from a higher base. Consequently, the UK's skills base will remain no better than average by international standards in 2020, with deficits across the board. This will have profound implications for the UK. As the global economy changes, the employment opportunities of the lowest skilled will continue to fall. UK businesses will find it increasingly difficult to compete in the new global economy, failing to innovate to take advantage of new opportunities abroad.

2.43   For the UK to succeed in the new global economy, it must commit to world class skills. Achieving this will require new, shared action with the Government, employers and individuals all taking increased responsibility, building on the promising successes of recent years. The Government must ensure a skills system that delivers economically valuable skills. Employers must exercise influence over a newly simplified system and increase their investment in skills, particularly for low skilled employees who too often do not benefit from training at present. Individuals must raise their sights, aspirations and motivation and invest in their own skills. Where skills were once *a* key lever for prosperity and fairness, they are now increasingly *the* key lever. The UK can only achieve world class prosperity and fairness if it achieves world class skills.

CONCLUSION

2.44   The UK's skills base has suffered from historic failings in the education and training systems. Over recent years, the UK's skills base has improved significantly. The proportion of adults with high skills has risen from 21 per cent in 1994 to 29 per cent in 2005. The proportion of adults with no qualifications has fallen from 22 to 13 per cent. Despite this, the UK's skills base remains mediocre by international standards.

2.45   The Government and Devolved Administrations have stretching targets to improve the skills of young people and adults in the UK. If these are met, they will bring significant improvements in the UK's skills base, reducing the number of people with low qualifications and increasing the numbers with high qualifications. Other countries are improving their skills too, often from a higher base. The Review's analysis shows the UK will fall short of being a world leader in skills in 2020. National prosperity and fairness will be increasingly constrained, with the UK unable to adapt to global economic changes.

---

[18] *Management practices across firms and nations*, Bloom, Dorgan, Van Reenan, Rippen, LSE-Mckinsey, 2005.

[19] *National Employer Skills Survey 2005*, Learning and Skills Council, 2006.

2.46   The responsibility for improving adult skills in the UK has long been shared between government, employers and individuals. The balance between the three has changed over time, with employers compelled to train their employees in the 1960s and 1970s, before a shift back to a more voluntary approach in the 1980s and 1990s.

2.47   The approaches that work involve employers and individuals having clear responsibilities and a system that follows demand from them rather than planning supply. Recent innovations that follow this approach are showing clear signs of success. There are some excellent Sector Skills Councils, allowing employers to articulate their needs and raise demand collectively. Train to Gain, providing flexible training in the workplace in England, is a clear success.

2.48   The Review has concluded that the UK must raise its sights and sets as its national goal a world class skills base. Delivering this ambition will require a new, shared commitment from the Government, employers and individuals, building on what works and changing what does not. The next chapter sets out the Review's recommendation for world class skills and a new partnership between the Government, employers and individuals to deliver it.

3 WORLD CLASS SKILLS

Chapter summary

Previous chapters revealed that the UK's historic skills deficit has constrained productivity, employment and social justice. They showed that significant improvements are being made in the UK's skills base but that the improvements also underway in other countries mean that the UK will remain average by international standards.

Delivering prosperity and fairness in the new global economy demands world class skills. The Review recommends a new national ambition for the UK to be a world leader in skills. This ambition should be benchmarked by the upper quartile of the OECD, equivalent to the top 8 of the 30 countries in the OECD. It will be based on principles of ensuring that every adult has a basic platform of skills, improving the quality of the UK's intermediate skills base and ensuring improvements at the top end drive improved management and innovation.

Putting these benchmarks and principles into practice, the Review recommends a commitment to achieve by 2020:

- **95 per cent of adults to have the basic skills of functional literacy and numeracy,** up from 85 per cent and 79 per cent respectively in 2005;
- **exceeding 90 per cent of adults qualified to at least Level 2,** up from 69 per cent in 2005. A commitment to achieve the Review's world class projection of 95 per cent as soon as possible;
- **shifting the balance of intermediate skills to Level 3.** Improving the esteem, quality and quantity of intermediate skills. An additional 1.9 million Level 3 attainments, including boosting the number of Apprentices to 500,000 a year; and
- **exceeding 40 per cent of adults qualified to Level 4 and above,** up from 29 per cent in 2005, with a commitment to achieving world class levels.

This ambition will require more than doubling projected rates of improvement at most skill levels. However, the prize for achieving it is large. It will deliver a possible net benefit of at least £80 billion over 30 years, an annual average of £2.5 billion. These benefits will flow from an increase of up to 10 per cent in the rate of productivity growth and accelerating projected growth in the employment rate by around 10 per cent. World class skills will also drive reductions in child poverty and inequality, building a fairer society.

Delivering this ambition and prize will require shared action between the Government, employers and individuals. The Review recommends a new partnership based on:

- **Government.** Investing more, focusing on the least skilled. Ensuring that the education system delivers a highly-skilled flow into the workforce. Creating a framework to ensure employers and individuals drive the skills system to deliver economically valuable skills. Being prepared to act on market failures, targeting help where it is needed most. Regulate if necessary and with care to reach the UK's skills ambitions;
- **employers.** Increasing their investment in skills to raise productivity, wherever possible increasing investment in portable accredited training. Ensuring the skills system delivers economically valuable skills by effectively influencing the system. Volunteering to support their low-skilled employees to reach at least a first, full Level 2. Introducing sectoral measures such as levies where a majority of employers in the sector agree; and
- **individuals.** Raising their aspirations and awareness. Demanding more of their employers. Investing more in their own skills development.

3.1   The previous chapters showed how the UK's historic skills deficit is being tackled, but that improvements in other countries mean the UK will still fall short of being a world leader in skills by 2020. This chapter sets out the Review's recommendation that the UK set its sights higher and become a world leader in skills. It sets out the principles on which shared action between the Government, employers and individuals to meet this ambition should be based, building on the progress in recent years.

A WORLD CLASS SKILLS BASE

3.2   As Chapter 2 showed, the UK is achieving significant improvements in its skills base. However, these will not be enough to make the UK a world leader in skills by 2020, as Chart 2.5 showed. Consequently, UK prosperity will remain constrained and fail to meet the challenge of globalisation. To rise to the challenge, the Review recommends a new ambition for the UK to achieve world class skills. The Review recommends moving the UK into the top eight in the world at each skill level by 2020, achieving the top quartile in the OECD.

3.3   This benchmark is based on qualifications. On the job training is a vital source of workforce development and not all training should be formal. However, focusing as much training as possible on qualifications, as long as qualifications reflect economically valuable skills, brings enormous benefits to both individuals and employers. Employers are prepared to pay significantly higher wages for those with qualifications. For example, the return to a degree is estimated at around 25 per cent and the returns to GCSEs are around 25 per cent.[1]

3.4   For individuals, they provide portability in the labour market, allowing them to demonstrate the skills they have acquired. For employers, they provide valuable signals when recruiting new workers and also motivate employees to complete their training. Qualifications form a major part of employer recruitment strategies, especially screening candidates prior to shortlisting or interview.[2] As a result, both individuals and employers value qualifications. The majority of individuals prefer studying towards a qualification[3] and over one half of employers feel it is quite or very important that the training provided leads to a qualification.[4]

Underpinning delivery   **3.5**   The Review has used the projections shown in Chart 2.5 as a benchmark for translating this ambition into objectives. There is great uncertainty over what world class will be in 2020. These projections, and the use of top quartile in the OECD, should not be taken too literally. Straight translation of the benchmark into UK targets does not work at every level of achievement. Focussing too much on a relative measure would lead to perverse outcomes as policy and ambitions in other countries change. The Review's recommendations have been informed by a view that:

- everyone should have a good grounding of basic skills and the wider platform of skills for employability represented by Level 2, recognising that there will always be a small proportion of people for whom these skills are not attainable;

- to improve the quality of the UK's intermediate skills base, the balance of intermediate skills in the adult population should shift from Level 2 to Level 3; and

---

[1] See, for example, *Returns to education: A non-technical summary of CEE work and policy discussion*, Sianesi, Institute for Fiscal Studies and Centre for the Economics of Education, 2003.

[2] *CIPD Recruitment, Retention and Turnover Survey*, 2006.

[3] *National Adult Learning Survey*, LSC, 2002.

[4] *The Market for Qualifications in the UK*, PWC, 2005.

- world class higher level skills should deliver improved management skills and innovation, as well as improving the proportion of people with a full Level 4 qualification or above.

World class skills **3.6** Using the OECD benchmark, the Review recommends the following ambitions for the UK by 2020:[5]

- 95 per cent of adults with the basic skills of functional literacy and numeracy;[6]

- exceeding 90 per cent of adults qualified to at least Level 2, up from 29 per cent in 2005, and with a commitment to achieving the Review's world class projection of 95 per cent as soon as is feasible;

- shifting the balance of intermediate skills from Level 2 to Level 3, more than doubling projected rates of adult attainment at Level 3, to achieve 1.9 million additional first Level 3s, including increasing the number of Apprentices to 500,000 a year, with most growth coming from adults; and

- exceeding 40 per cent of the adult population to have Level 4 or above, up from 29 per cent today, with a commitment to achieving world class levels.

3.7 Meeting this ambition will require a dramatic acceleration in anticipated rates of attainment at all skill levels as well as a step change in the quality and use of these skills. Later chapters set out the Review's plans for meeting them and the respective roles of the Government, employers, trades unions and individuals.

Devolved **3.8** This is a UK ambition responding to a global challenge on economic performance, **Administrations** employment and productivity. All parts of the UK need to raise their game. Skills policy in the UK is devolved. The Review has worked closely with the administrations from Scotland, Wales and Northern Ireland in developing its ambitions. The Devolved Administrations (DAs), as well as the UK Government, are considering the implications of the Review's recommendations for their policies and targets. In Scotland, the themes of this report will now be taken into and debated under the auspices of the Scottish Executive's consultation *Lifelong Learning – Building Success: A discussion of specific issues related to lifelong learning in Scotland*, published in November 2006.

THE IMPACT OF WORLD CLASS SKILLS

3.9 The Review has analysed the costs of delivering the world class ambition for skills and the scale of the benefits that meeting this ambition would have for the economy, businesses and individuals in the UK.

The cost of world class skills

3.10 The previous section set out the scale of acceleration required to deliver world class skills by 2020. It is clearly very difficult to accurately model skills profiles 15 years ahead and so there is a great deal of uncertainty over the precise figures. However, the Review's projections give a sense of the scale of the change required to be a world leader in skills between 2007 and 2020:

---

[5] Adults means those aged 19 to State Pension age.

[6] Defined as Level 1 literacy (equivalent to GCSE English at grade D-G) and Entry Level 3 numeracy (one level below Level 1).

- a total of 7.4 million adult basic skills attainments, compared with the current Skills for Life target of 2.25 million attainments between 2001 and 2010;

- up to 5.7 million adults achieving a first Level 2 qualification, compared with current projections to 2020 of 4.1 million;

- a total of 4 million adults achieving a first Level 3 qualification, compared with current projections to 2020 of 2.1 million; and

- a total of 5.5 million adults achieving at least a first Level 4 qualification, across the whole workforce.

3.11 It is extremely difficult to estimate the cost of achieving this change. The overall additional cost will depend on factors including: whether current Government targets are met; how accurate the Review's projections for the likely path of skills improvements prove to be; and the unit cost of delivering each qualification. Each is highly uncertain. For example, qualifications delivered through Train to Gain and online tend to be cheaper than those delivered in Further Education (FE) colleges. The mix of delivery channels will change over time.

3.12 The Government is committed to increasing the share of GDP devoted to education over the lifetime of this Parliament. Spending on skills will benefit as a result of this commitment. The level of ambition set out in this report will require additional investment by the State, employers and individuals. The Review recognises that greater efficiency in delivery, economies of scale and rationalisation in the skills landscape should reduce these costs.

3.13 This report recommends the optimal level of skills in the economy. The Review estimates that additional annual investment in skills up to Level 3 will need to rise to around £1.5-£2 billion by 2020 if the UK is to achieve world class status at basic and intermediate levels. In addition, increased investment is required in higher education (HE) to achieve world class status. Uncertainties over HE participation data and unstable trends across much of the OECD, make it problematic to provide accurate costings for world class levels. There will be a review of funding arrangements for HE in 2009.

3.14 It is vital that the necessary reforms and capacity are in place to make best use of any additional investment, for example, to ensure that the additional qualifications are economically valuable. Increased investment should be phased in carefully over time to ensure that value for money is maintained.

Balance of responsibility **3.15** The costs must be shared between the Government, individuals and employers. As the Review's interim report set out, government investment in skills should be focused on ensuring everyone has the opportunity to build a platform of skills and tackling market failures. It set out evidence that there are key market failures at all skill levels, but that these are most prevalent at the bottom end. This suggests that government funding should be focused on low skills, and that responsibility should be shared with employers and individuals further up, where there are clear private returns. Box 3.1 discusses market failures in skills in more detail.

literacy and numeracy skills by 2020, matching the best in the world.[8] The current basic skills position, that which the UK is on track to achieve and the Leitch Review's proposals are shown in Chart 3.1.

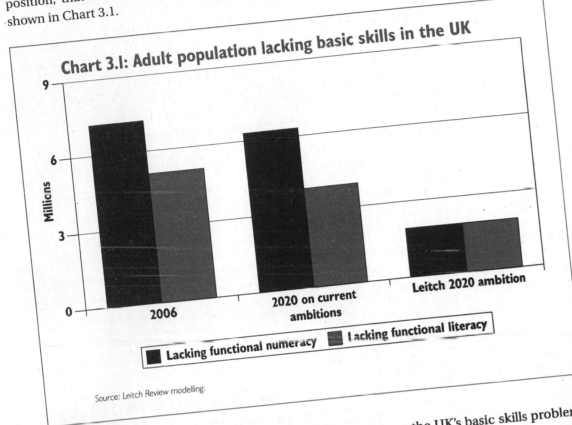

Chart 3.1: Adult population lacking basic skills in the UK

Source: Leitch Review modelling.

3.33 Achieving the Review's recommendation would mean the UK's basic skills problems are no longer a key deficit in its skills base. The massive benefits of achieving this, in improved productivity, employment and fairness, were set out above. This would still leave large numbers of people in the UK lacking functional literacy and numeracy. However, the UK would achieve a step change in its performance and be world class in comparison to other countries. The top performing countries in the OECD International Adult Literacy Survey (IALS) had at least 90 per cent of the working age population with functional literacy skills. Younger people, who will still be of working age in 2020, scored even higher. Just five per cent of those aged 26 to 35 in Sweden lacked functional literacy skills. The top countries in IALS had at least 90 per cent with functional numeracy but, once again, these are expected to improve by 2020 to in excess of 95 per cent – in line with the Review's ambition for the UK.

world **3.34** The Skills for Life survey showed that a substantial proportion of adults with Level 2
skills and above qualifications lack basic skills. Qualifications gained, while potentially contributing to improved basic skills, are not the best measure of basic skills in the UK. The Review recommends that progress to the new national objective of 95 per cent of the adult population having functional literacy and numeracy skills by 2020 be measured through a Skills for Life Survey every two years. This is a fundamentally different target, based on measuring outcomes in the population rather than the outputs of the skills system. Progress will be measured by tests of actual skills among adults, rather than through attainment of qualifications.

Where functional literacy is defined as Level 1 and functional numeracy is defined as Entry Level 3.

Box 3.1: Market failures in skills

Market failures occur in various aspects of the wider market for skills. These are likely to create problems that government policy should address. The main areas of market failure are as follows:

Time preference and risk. These are short-termist attitudes to investment in skills and their future returns by employers or individuals. Investing in skills is a risk; neither individuals nor employers can be certain of the benefits they will gain if they invest in training. Both may be concerned they will not receive a sufficient return, or may prefer to do other things with their time.

Credit market failure. This occurs when individuals or firms are not able to borrow the costs of training, even where this training would most likely deliver a positive return. It can be more difficult to secure loans against human capital than other forms of investment. Individuals and firms may lack the necessary credit history to acquire loans and so be unable to invest in skills that would benefit them in the longer term.

Information failure. This occurs when the information available to individuals or firms is incomplete or imperfect, or when some have more of different information to others. This might be awareness of the benefits of skills improvements, or information about the quality and content of particular courses and particular institutions.

Externalities. These are social costs or benefits of decisions that are felt more broadly than just through returns to individuals or firms. An individual or business will make decisions on investment in skills based on their assessment of the costs and benefits to themselves. They will not take full account of any wider benefits to society or spillover effects on other firms.

The evidence shows that these market failures are more likely to impact at the lower end, meaning that government intervention is most justified in low skills. However, market failures, particularly externalities, also occur at the higher skills end.

3.16 The Review's interim report showed that the existing balance of responsibility for funding training is extremely complex and varies according to status, age and type of study. The Review recommends a much clearer financial balance of responsibility, based on clear principles of government funding targeted at market failure and responsibility shared according to economic benefit. In practice this means for the additional cost of a raised ambition:

- the Government should provide the bulk of funding for basic and Level 2 skills, with employers cooperating to ensure employees are able to achieve these skills;

- for higher intermediate skills (Level 3) employers and individuals should make a much higher contribution, in the order of at least 50 per cent; and

- at Level 4 and above, individuals and employers should pay the bulk of the costs as they will benefit most.

3.17 Where the Government does invest, funding must meet employers and individuals needs, within this framework of a balance of responsibilities.

The benefits of world class skills

'The Prize' **3.18** The Review has found that achieving a world class skills base will deliver massive benefits to the UK economy, through higher productivity and employment. It will also lead to reduced inequality and poverty and increased social mobility. These benefits will be shared by individuals, employers and society.

3.19 The Review's interim report introduced a Cost Benefit Analysis (CBA) model, which the Review has developed to quantify some of these benefits. This showed that the benefits of investing in skills clearly and significantly outweigh the costs, even under cautious assumptions. It showed that investment in basic skills delivers the biggest returns, equivalent to more than £4 for every £1 invested. High skills drive innovation and leadership, but these gains cannot be realised unless the workforce has the platform of skills and flexibility to adapt and change. More detail on the model and its results can be found in the interim report.

3.20 The Review has found that helping people with low skills improve their skills can help to significantly reduce income inequality and child poverty. While it was not possible to quantify some of the wider benefits of skills discussed in Chapter 1, such as improved health and reduced crime, these are also concentrated at the low skills end. Investing in intermediate and high skills results in large productivity benefits for the UK.

National benefits **3.21** The Review has used the CBA model to analyse the scale of the potential impacts of achieving the world class skills base it is recommending. Achieving a world class base will deliver a possible overall net benefit of at least £80 billion over 30 years, equivalent to an average of £2.5 billion each year, even taking into account the significant costs of delivering it and on the basis of cautious assumptions.

3.22 These benefits would come from a combination of increased productivity growth and higher employment. The Review's analysis suggests that the annual rate of productivity growth would rise by around 0.1 percentage points from its current underlying trend of 2 per cent. This is a rise in the underlying growth rate of productivity of 5-10 per cent, equivalent to an average of £1 to 2 billion of output per year.

3.23 The Review's model makes the cautious assumption that a person's productivity is equal to the wages that they earn. In reality, as set out in Chapter 1, this is likely to be a significant underestimate. Based on these studies, productivity growth could accelerate by up to 15 per cent, equivalent to an average of up to £2.5 billion each year. As a result of increased productivity, output per worker, the key measure of productivity and prosperity, would be around 4 per cent higher in 2020 than it would otherwise be, equivalent to £1,800 to £2,200 per worker today.

3.24 In addition, based on conservative assumptions, an additional 200,000 people would be in work by 2020, raising the employment rate by at least 0.2 percentage points and contributing to the Government's aspiration of an 80 per cent employment rate. This is equivalent to an increase of 0.02 percentage points each year. To put this into context, the Government projects annual growth in the employment rate of 0.2 percentage point each year.[7] Achieving world class skills could therefore accelerate the growth of the employment rate by 10 per cent, a very significant acceleration.

Benefits to **3.25** Businesses will share significantly in these benefits. The significant acceleration in **businesses** productivity growth will give them a much more productive workforce. Ensuring that everyone gains a good platform of basic and employability skills will expand the pool of

[7] *Trend growth: recent developments and prospects*, HM Treasury, 2002.

potential workers that businesses can choose from. Enhancing the availability of training and skilled workers will also help businesses to manage the challenge of globalisation and technological change, enhancing their flexibility.

3.26 A more highly-skilled labour force will enable businesses to innovate further, taking advantage of new technologies and ways of working in order to improve productivity and capture new markets. Without this, businesses will become increasingly vulnerable to global competition, finding it difficult to take advantage of new markets and increasingly difficult to retain share in their current market.

Benefits to **3.27** Building a world class skills base will enhance employment and pay prospects, **individuals** leading to at least an additional 200,000 people being in work. As the global economy changes, the employment prospects of the least skilled will continue to decline. The structure of the UK economy will also change. Unless people are equipped with flexible skills and are willing to retrain, they will not be able to move into growth industries and take new opportunities. Equipping them with these skills will help to deliver improved economic security in the new global economy.

Costs of inaction **3.28** The benefits from acting are large, but the consequences of inaction are also large and very disturbing. The UK would fail to accelerate productivity growth and lack the skills ba[se] needed to take advantage of the opportunities that globalisation brings. Businesses wo[uld] lack the workers to grow and expand in an increasingly competitive global econ[omy]. Individuals lacking the skills and flexibility to move into new work would risk be[coming] detached from labour market opportunity – a lost generation.

MAKING THE UK A WORLD LEADER IN SKILLS

3.29 This section sets out the Review's ambition for world class skills in mor[e detail by] skill level.

Basic skills

The current **3.30** Nowhere is the UK's skills deficit more apparent than in basic [skills.] **situation** 5 million adults lack functional literacy, the level needed to get by i[n work and] million adults lack functional numeracy skills. As Chapter 2 showe[d, the UK performs] poorly internationally. The Government is on track to improve th[is situation] but will less than halve the scale of the problem by 2020. Even [by 2020, the number] of Swedes lacked functional literacy, compared with the 10 p[er cent the UK hopes to] achieve by 2020.

3.31 Basic skills are highly valued in the labour marke[t. People with] such skills are far more likely to be in work, more produ[ctive] mean that the job opportunities of those with basic sk[ills are] limited. Without functional literacy and numeracy [it will be increasingly] difficult to do their jobs effectively and to progress[. Future employment and] prosperity will increasingly depend on.

World class basic **3.32** Unless the UK tackles its basic skills d[eficit, an entire] **skills** generation, with millions of adults ever mo[re] chances severely curtailed. If the UK were t[o] the number of adults lacking basic literac[y] basic numeracy to 6.3 million by 2020[ ] efforts must be more than trebled, s[o]

Achievin[g a world]
class basi[c skills]

3.35 The Review recommends achieving this new national objective through improvements for both young people and adults. Ensuring that everyone leaving school has the basic literacy and numeracy skills they will need in life is critical. It is unacceptable in the 21st century in the fifth richest country in the world for young people to leave school lacking these basics. Yet over one in six young people in England do. The UK must avoid a new generation leaving school without basic skills. Reforms to embed functional literacy and numeracy in maths and English GCSEs must succeed. In 2006 just 45 per cent of school leavers achieved five or more grades A* to C, including English and mathematics, at GCSE or equivalent. This must rise dramatically so that all young people leave school with the basic platform of skills they need to succeed and progress.

3.36 More than 70 per cent of the UK's working age population in 2020 are already over the age of 16. Consequently, even if all young people gain good literacy and numeracy skills from now, the UK would still be left with a huge basic skills problem in 2020. **The Review proposes to more than treble the rate at which basic skills deficits in the adult population are currently being tackled.** This will involve improving the literacy skills of around 2 million adults more than will be achieved under current projections by 2020 and the numeracy of an additional 4.6 million adults. This should be delivered through both specific basic skills qualifications and 'embedding' functional literacy and numeracy within other qualifications.

Skills and the labour market **3.37** People entering the labour market, whether from full-time education or worklessness, also need a wider set of skills, such as IT, communications and team working. These wider employability skills should be embedded within training and qualifications, as well as being taught separately as appropriate. Chapter 7 sets out proposals to ensure that those who are out of work are able to gain the skills they need to find work, stay in employment and progress. The English for Speakers of Other Languages (ESOL) programme will also be important for helping those coming to the UK succeed.

Platform of skills

3.38 The UK's current skills problems are most severe at the bottom end. The UK trails far behind key comparators in terms of the proportion of adults with the equivalent of a decent school leaving qualification. In 2005, around one in three adults aged 25 to 64, 9.7 million people, lacked a Level 2 qualification in the UK, more than double the proportions in the USA, Japan, Canada, Sweden and Germany. Even if current challenging projections are met, around 10 per cent of the adult population will lack at least this level of qualification in 2020, leaving the UK still behind key comparators.

World class platform of skills **3.39** It is essential that all adults are able to achieve a platform of skills for entry into, and retention and progression within, work and the labour market. **The Review recommends that the UK commit to exceeding 90 per cent of the adult population qualified to at least Level 2 by 2020, up from 69 per cent in 2005, and achieving the world class level of 95 per cent as soon as possible.** Alongside this, the flow into the labour force must match world class standards. It is likely, given the better qualification profile of younger age groups, that the 95 per cent ambition will be reached earlier than for the adult population as a whole. The Government should give consideration to this. Chart 3.2 shows the scale of change needed.

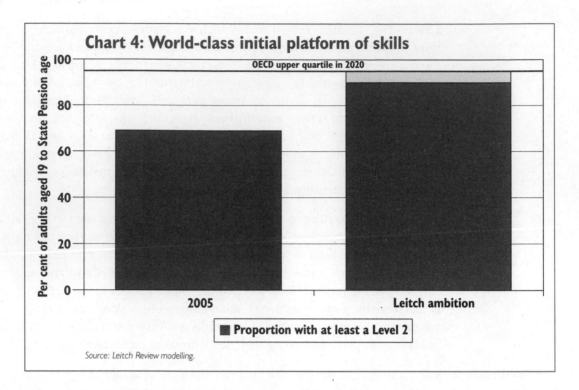

Chart 4: World-class initial platform of skills

Source: Leitch Review modelling.

Ensuring qualifications deliver value

3.40 Current improvements in the number of adults with a Level 2 qualification are driven by the Government's target, set out in Chapter 2, to reduce the number of adults in the workforce lacking this level of qualification by 40 per cent by 2010. Given the rate of improvement to date, this will be an extremely challenging target to meet. The Review has heard many representations proposing that this target be dropped. It has heard arguments that the low and in some cases non-existent wage returns to many Level 2 qualifications show that they are not valued by people or employers.

3.41 Qualifications must reflect skills that individuals and employers value for improvements in the UK's comparative qualifications profile to improve its effective skills base. Level 2 can provide an effective platform from which people can progress and it will increasingly be the minimum standard expected for employability as the economy changes. Level 2 qualifications delivered in the workplace have significant wage returns. Chapter 4 sets out recommendations to ensure all qualifications, including at Level 2, deliver skills valued by employers and individuals. These reforms will ensure that a target for increasing attainment at Level 2 by 2020 will deliver real economic value.

Intermediate skills

3.42 Many representations to the Review have focused on the weakness of the UK's intermediate skills base. It is difficult to compare intermediate skills internationally. For the purposes of such comparisons, the OECD considers both Level 2 and Level 3 qualifications in the UK to be intermediate level. However, many international comparator countries tend to describe Level 3 (upper secondary level) as intermediate because it typically corresponds to the main school leaving level, such as the Diploma in Secondary Studies in Canada and the Higher School Certificate in Australia. Broadly, these are equivalent to A Levels or Level 3 in the new 14-19 Diplomas currently in development. Unlike the UK, most countries do not have a school leaving certificate at age 16.

The current situation

3.43 Even with a definition that includes Level 2, the UK fares poorly, ranking 20th out of the 30 countries in the OECD, as was shown in Chart 2.1. To a large extent, this is the result of the relatively high proportion of people in the UK lacking a Level 2 qualification. As Chapter l discussed, this stems from both historically low proportions of young people gaining GCSEs or their equivalent at school and low rates of attainment of these level of qualifications among adults.

3.44   Poor progression from Level 2 to Level 3, both at school and in the workforce, also limits the quality of the UK's intermediate skills base. Fewer young people in the UK stay on in education or training past the age of 16 than in many other countries. With 83 per cent of 17 year-olds in education or training in 2004, the UK ranked 20th out of 30 OECD countries, below the OECD average of 85 per cent. In Japan, South Korea, Finland and Sweden, more than 93 per cent of 17-year-olds are in some form of education or training, even though the age for completing compulsory education is under 17 years of age. In Sweden, 95 per cent of all 18 year olds are still enrolled in secondary education.[9]

World class **3.45**   The Review recommends that the UK commit to achieving a world class
intermediate intermediate skills base, shifting the balance from Level 2 to Level 3. This will drive increased
skills productivity, improve people's pay prospects and better equip both employers and employees to adapt to change. Delivering the ambition should include employers committing to boosting the number of Apprentices to 500,000, with most of the growth coming from adults to drive progression in the workforce.

3.46   The ambition set out earlier to exceed 90 per cent of the adult population with at least a Level 2 qualification, moving to 95 per cent as soon as possible, will mean that the UK's intermediate skills base is of a world class size and ensure that all have the platform of skills increasingly needed. To improve the quality of intermediate skills, the Review recommends more than doubling current rates of progression by adults to Level 3, an additional 1.9 million Level 3s. The outcomes of this are shown in Chart 3.3 below and compared to the current situation and projections for 2020. The third column in the chart illustrates the 2020 scenario if the UK just pursued the world-class platform of skills. The balance between Level 2 and Level 3 is skewed towards Level 2 as a result. Increasing Level 3 attainments by an additional 1.9 million attainments, shown in the fourth column, rebalances the Level 2 and Level 3 split, reflecting the importance of Level 3 skills.

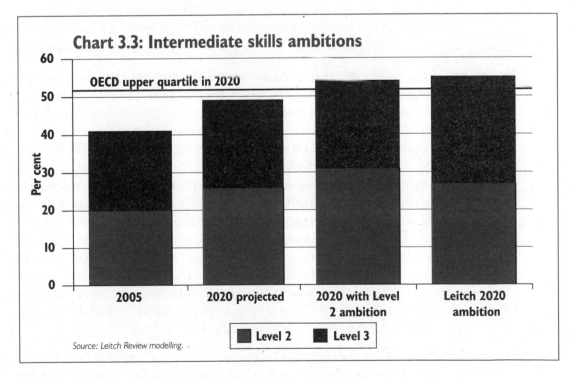

Chart 3.3: Intermediate skills ambitions

Source: Leitch Review modelling.

---

[9] *Education at a glance*, OECD, 2006.

Achieving world class intermediate skills   **3.47**   To reach this ambition, the Review recognises that there must be a step change in attainment of intermediate both skills at school and in the labour force. The Government has already set an ambition to raise participation in education in England after the age of 16 from 75 per cent today to 90 per cent by 2015.

14-19 reform   **3.48**   Despite recent improvements, the UK's post-16 participation in education and training is below the OECD average. International evidence suggests that parity of esteem of the vocational route and a smoothing of the current break point at age 16 are needed to achieve world-leading levels of post-16 participation in education and training. The new specialised Diplomas in England are critical to increasing participation in education and training for all young people.

3.49   The 14-19 Reform Programme must successfully deliver a fully integrated 14-19 phase, including curriculum, funding and financial support; and must ensure appropriate stretch and breadth in A levels. The 2008 Review of progress as set out in the 14-19 White Paper published in February 2005, will be important in identifying what more can be done to achieve these objectives. Once the Government is on track to successfully deliver Diplomas, with rising participation at age 17 and significant improvement in OECD rankings, it should implement a change in the law, so that all young people must remain in full or part-time education or workplace training up to the age of 18.

3.50   The Review recommends that the Government work with employers to deliver more than a doubling of attainment at Level 3 by adults, including increasing the number of Apprentices in the UK to 500,000 a year. Sector Skills Councils (SSCs) should draw up Sector Skills Agreements (SSAs) that include firm targets for employers to increase their investment in intermediate skills, including Apprenticeships. More details are included in Chapter 5.

High skills

3.51   Chapter 1 showed that high skills are becoming increasingly important in the global economy. They drive growth, facilitate innovation and are crucial for world-class management and leadership. As the global economy changes, a country's economic prospects will increasingly depend on their skills base – advanced economies such as the UK must succeed on the skills of their people rather than on labour costs alone.

The current situation   **3.52**   The UK has massively expanded the number of young people going to university in the past 20 years. The Government has set the challenging target to move towards 50 per cent participation in HE by those aged 18 to 30. As a consequence, the proportion of the UK adult population qualified to at least Level 4 has risen from 19 per cent in 1994 to 29 per cent today. However, other countries are going further and faster. The proportion of people aged 25 to 64 and qualified to Level 4 or above in both the US and Canada is around 40 per cent today. The wage returns that people with a degree get have remained steady over the past decade indicating that the increased supply of people with high skills has been met with increased demand.[10]

---

[10] *Further analysis of the returns to academic and vocational qualifications*, McIntosh, CEE, 2004.

3.53 Funding for HE in the UK from both public and private sources is low by international standards – less than one half that in the USA and 40 per cent lower than in Sweden. The UK currently spends 1.1 per cent of GDP, of which around three quarters is from public sources. This compares to overall funding of 2.9 per cent in the US, 2.6 per cent in South Korea and 2.4 per cent in Canada. Funding has not increased in line with the number of students. Consequently, funding per student has halved in the UK over the past 20 years, although it has been sustained over the last decade. Although higher than the OECD average, per student funding in the UK ($11,866) is around half the US level of investment ($24,704) and substantially lower than Canada ($19,992) and Sweden ($16,073).[11]

50 per cent target for HE participation

3.54 The increase in the proportion of people qualified to Level 4 has been driven by the Government's target to move towards 50 per cent of those aged 18-30 participating in HE by 2010. As noted above, this is not unusual in international terms with many countries, such as Canada, going further. Participation has remained at around 43 per cent in recent years, leading people to challenge the attainability of a 50 per cent participation rate.

3.55 The 50 per cent target has provided an incentive for the HE sector to focus on increasing the number of young people going to university. However, some of this focus has been at the expense of engaging with employers and increasing workforce development. Moreover, the target tends to prioritise first full degrees and traditional undergraduate study, where funding levels are higher, ahead of part-time opportunities for employees and more focused high skills courses that reflect the needs of employers. Finally, it focuses on participation in higher education rather than actual attainment.

3.56 Concentrating too much on younger age groups could create further longer term problems for the amount and the use of high level skills in our workforce. With more young people qualified to this level and fewer older people, it increases the likelihood of poor deployment of higher-level skills with relatively under-skilled owners, managers and leaders unable to find the best uses for new graduate recruits. As the Higher Education White Paper stated, new higher education growth should not be 'more of the same', based on traditional three year honours degrees. Rather provision should be based on new types of programme offering specific, job-related skills such as Foundation Degrees.

World class high skills

3.57 Calculations from the Review's international projections of skills, as shown in Chart 2.5, suggest that world-class high skills in 2020 would require 45 per cent of the population aged 19 to State Pension age qualified to at least Level 4. Projections at the high skill level are more uncertain than at other levels because of the amount of change in the underlying trend in the last decade across much of the OECD.

3.58 Sustaining current trends in HE will be incredibly challenging. If it were achieved, around 40 per cent of the UK's adult population would be qualified at Level 4 or above by 2020, compared to 29 per cent in 2005. This would be highly significant progress. However, to move the UK into the top quartile of OECD countries for high skills, will require the UK to set its sights higher. Achieving such an ambition will be extremely stretching and likely to be more stretching than the drive to increase the number of young people going to university. Achieving the broader workforce target will need to be underpinned by action to ensure a high flow of young people into HE, by moving toward 50 per cent of young people participating in HE.

---

[11] *Education at a glance* 2006, OECD, 2006.

3.59 The Review recommends that the UK commit to achieving world class high skills by 2020. The UK must commit now to exceeding 40 per cent of the population aged 19 to State Pension age qualified to Level 4 or above by 2020, and ensure that this ambition is updated so that the UK achieves world class high skills by 2020 as the nature of a world class ambition becomes clearer. The Commission and the Government should review the definition of world class high skills.

3.60 Growth of this order is unlikely to be achievable by trying to expand further the current model of HE. There are limits in capacity, and also limits to how far the current HE model can fully meet the expectations of the greater volume of employers and employees who would need to be attracted. Further improvements in the UK's high skills base must come from workforce development and increased employer engagement.

3.61 The UK's ambition has to be to raise the proportion of people with high skills across the labour force – through more young adults equipped with the skills they need for successful working lives, and through creating opportunities, through their employers, for the many people in work who have the potential to acquire high skills. This is why the Review recommends a rebalancing of the priorities of HE institutions to make available relevant, flexible and responsive provision that meets the high skills needs of employers and their staff.

3.62 Stimulating high skills acquisition within the workforce will require closer collaboration between HE institutions and employers and employees, especially for part time students and bespoke programmes. Chapter 4 sets out proposals to ensure universities are appropriately incentivised to deliver improvements in high level skills throughout the workforce and to increase employer investment in high skills. The Government is reviewing tuition fees for undergraduates in 2009.

3.63 The number of young people going to university must remain a major contributor toward a high skill workforce. Achieving the broader workforce target must be underpinned by success in helping more young people to go university, by moving toward 50 per cent of young people participating in higher education. It is critical that access to university is dramatically improved so that young people from all backgrounds have a fair chance of attending. This will require action from universities and the Office for Fair Access to improve access and from the Government to raise awareness and aspirations among all young people and ensure standards in all schools continue to rise.

Postgraduate Skills

3.64 One of the most powerful levers for improving productivity will be higher level skills. Postgraduate, or Level 5 skills, such as MBAs and PhDs, can provide significant returns to organisations, individuals and to the economy as a whole. These higher level skills are key drivers of innovation, entrepreneurship, management, leadership and research and development. All of these are critical to a high skills, high performance economy and increasingly in demand from high performance, global employers. Level 5 skills should also be an important feature of greater employer collaboration with HE, as recommended in Richard Lambert's Review of Business – University Collaboration and described in more detail in Chapters 4 and 5.[12]

3.65 A target for Level 5 skills is not considered to be appropriate at this stage, but more attention should be given to monitoring the stock and flow of such skills in the economy. These skills will be increasingly essential to ensure the UK is at the forefront of global innovation and for sources of future growth and prosperity. The Government, together with

---

[12] *Lambert Review of Business-University Collaboration*, HM Treasury, 2003.

the Commission for Employment and Skills (see Chapter 4) and appropriate SSCs should take account of the supply of such skills and consider how best to increase the demand for Level 5 skills.

DELIVERING WORLD CLASS SKILLS

3.66 If the UK wants to have a world class skills base, it must aim for world class attainment among young people. There have been significant improvements in standards in schools. There is much further to go to ensure all young people leave school with the basic platform of skills they need and to make sure the proportion of people staying in education or training past the age of 16 matches the best in the world.

Adults **3.67** Improving the skills of young people, while essential, cannot be the sole solution to achieving world class skills. More than 70 per cent of the 2020 working age population are already over the age of 16. As the global economy changes and working lives lengthen as the population ages, adults will increasingly need to update their skills in the workforce. There is a pressing need to raise the rates of skills improvements among adults – the UK simply cannot reach a world class ambition without this.

3.68 For the benefits of world class skills to be realised, the Review recommends the following principles underpin their delivery:

- **shared responsibility.** Employers, individuals and the Government must increase action and investment. Employers and individuals should contribute most where they derive the greatest private returns. Government investment must focus on market failures, ensuring a basic platform of skills for all, targeting help where it is needed most;

- **focus on economically valuable skills.** Skill developments must provide real returns for individuals, employers and society. Wherever possible, skills should be portable to deliver mobility in the labour market for individuals and employers;

- **demand-led skills.** The skills system must meet the needs of individuals and employers. Vocational skills must be demand-led rather than centrally planned;

- **adapt and respond.** No one can accurately predict future demand for particular skill types. The framework must adapt and respond to future market needs; and

- **build on existing structures.** Don't always chop and change. Instead, improve the performance of current structures through simplification and rationalisation, stronger performance management and clearer remits. Continuity is important.

A new **3.69** Since 1945 debate has polarised around whether the Government needs to regulate
partnership to increase employer investment in training. The Review recommends a new partnership approach, building on the success of recent initiatives to build a more demand-led system, meeting the new challenges the UK faces through common action. In practice, this means:

- **Government**, investing more, focusing on the least skilled. Ensuring that the education system delivers a highly-skilled flow into the workforce. Creating a framework to ensure employers and individuals drive the skills system to deliver economically valuable skills. Being prepared to act on market failures, targeting help where it is most needed. Regulate if necessary and with care to reach the UK's skills ambitions;

- **employers**, to increase their investment in skills to impact productivity, wherever possible increasing investment in portable accredited training. Ensuring the skills system delivers economically valuable skills by effectively influencing the system. Pledging to support their low-skilled employees to reach at least a first full Level 2. Introducing sectoral measures, such as levies, where a majority of employers in the sector agree; and

- **individuals**, raising their aspirations and awareness. Demanding more of their employers. Investing more in their own skills development.

3.70   The next chapter sets out the Review's recommendations to build a fully demand-led skills system, essential if the skills delivered in the UK are to be economically valuable.

CONCLUSION

3.71   Previous chapters set out the clear and pressing case for improving the UK's skills base further and faster than is currently projected in order to improve both prosperity and fairness in a changing global environment.

3.72   This chapter has set out the Review's recommendations for a shared national commitment to world class skills. It has discussed what this means at each skill level, more than doubling projected rates of improvement, as well as the need for clear action to improve the quality of skills and how they are used in the workplace. It has also set out how progress toward this ambition should be benchmarked and recommendations for Government targets and aims.

3.73   Achieving the Review's ambition will bring huge and lasting benefits to the UK economy, a possible net benefit of at least £80 billion over 30 years, equivalent to an annual average of £2.5 billion. This would come through boosting productivity growth by up to 15 per cent, leaving the average UK worker producing at least £1,800 more of output each year in 2020 than would otherwise be the case, and boosting projected growth in the employment rate by up to 10 per cent, helping an additional 200,000 people into work.

3.74   These benefits will be shared. Businesses will gain a more productive workforce and larger pool of skilled labour. Individuals will gain better job and pay prospects. Society will be both more prosperous and fairer. The responsibility for achieving world class skills must also be shared. The next chapter sets out the Review's recommendations for reforming the skills and qualifications systems to ensure they deliver economically relevant skills that employers and individuals need.

4 A DEMAND LED SKILLS SYSTEM

Chapter summary

The previous chapter set out the Review's proposals for a shared national mission for the UK to be a world leader in skills, delivered through new shared action between the Government, employers, trades unions and individuals. Chapter 2 set out the historically weak track record of planning skills provision and the need for this ambition to be delivered through a demand-led system. This chapter sets out the Review's recommendations to build on achievements to date and make the skills system fully demand led, so it flexibly delivers the skills employers and individuals need.

There have been significant successes in making the skills system more demand-led. Train to Gain is delivering training flexibly and is popular with employers and employees. Sector Skills Councils (SSC) are showing encouraging signs of better engaging employers. Despite this, representations to the Review have highlighted the complexity and bureaucracy of the system for delivering skills and its continuing reliance on planning supply rather than meeting the needs of customers. They also highlighted the complexity of the qualification system – there are over 22,000 qualifications in the UK and too many of these, particularly at lower levels, are little valued by individuals or employers. These problems have constrained investment in skills by employers and individuals.

The Review has developed recommendations to make the system fully demand-led and focused on economically valuable skills:

- **demand-led funding.** Route the great majority of public funding for adult vocational skills in England through Train to Gain and Learner Accounts by 2010. On adult skills, a major streamlining of the Learning and Skills Council to focus on managing Train to Gain and Learner Accounts, processing funding and ensuring effective provider competition;

- **strengthen employer voice.** Rationalise existing bodies, strengthen the collective voice and better articulate employer views on skills by creating a new Commission for Employment and Skills, reporting to central Government and the devolved administrations. The Commission will be responsible for managing the employer voice on skills, within a national framework of individual rights; and

- **ensuring qualifications reflect economically valuable skills.** Qualifications must reflect the skills employers' value. The Review recommends that employers, through their SSCs, should be more responsible for the control of vocational qualifications. Only vocational qualifications approved by SSCs will be eligible for public funding.

These recommendations will deliver a radically simplified system, with improved economic returns at every level. They will help to transform providers of adult skills, requiring them to deliver economically valuable outcomes. They will put employers and trade unions at the heart of scrutinising the system to make sure it lives up to this vision.

4.1   Chapter 2 set out the Review's recommendation that the UK set a shared national ambition for world class skills and the large benefits, in improved prosperity and fairness, this will bring. These benefits will only be fully realised if the ambition is based on economically valuable skills. Chapter 2 showed that this will only happen if the skills system is demand-led. This chapter sets out the Review's proposals to build on successful reforms to date and build a fully demand-led skills system.

A DEMAND-LED SKILLS SYSTEM

4.2   As Chapter 2 set out, previous approaches to delivering skills have been too 'supply driven', based on the Government asking employers to articulate their needs and then planning supply to meet this. This approach has a historically weak track record. Employers are confused by the plethora of advisory, strategic and planning bodies they are asked to input to. Under a planned system, the incentives are for providers to continue doing what they have done in the past so long as they meet planning requirements, rather than responding flexibly as demand changes. As a result, less than 10 per cent of employer training is in FE.

The current   **4.3**   In England, post-16 provision is planned, funded and secured by the Learning and **system**   Skills Council (LSC), in partnership with Regional Skills Partnerships (RSPs) and colleges, providers and other key stakeholders. Scotland, Wales and Northern Ireland, with very different systems, rely on planning provision, together with employer input. In Wales, all funding for further and higher education is managed by the Welsh Assembly Government, through the Higher Education Funding Council Wales (HEFCW), and directly for other funding. In Scotland, all funding for further and higher education is distributed through the newly merged Scottish Funding Council for Further and Higher Education. In Northern Ireland, all funding for both further and higher education is distributed directly from the Department for Education and Learning Northern Ireland (DELNI). Chart 4.1 illustrates the current system in England.

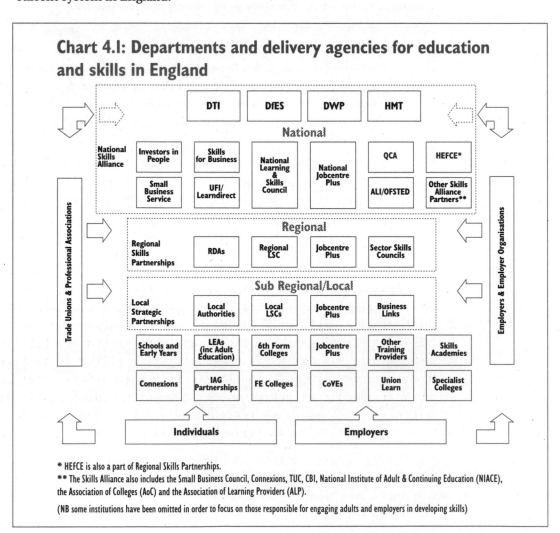

Chart 4.1: Departments and delivery agencies for education and skills in England

* HEFCE is also a part of Regional Skills Partnerships.

** The Skills Alliance also includes the Small Business Council, Connexions, TUC, CBI, National Institute of Adult & Continuing Education (NIACE), the Association of Colleges (AoC) and the Association of Learning Providers (ALP).

(NB some institutions have been omitted in order to focus on those responsible for engaging adults and employers in developing skills)

4.4   As Chapter 2 set out, the LSC has a total budget of some £10 billion, of which around £3 billion is for adult skills. The LSC plans provision with colleges and other providers through a network of 47 local LSCs. Current plans are to replace these with a new regional tier of councils managing 148 local partnership teams. The LSC allocates funding on the basis of expected demand. If demand does not meet expectations, funding for subsequent years is adjusted. This can mean that colleges aim to 'recruit' employers and individuals into planned courses to fill places, rather than responding flexibly to demand. The LSC is also responsible for planning and funding provision for those aged 16-19, within a strategy that is jointly developed and implemented with Local Authorities (LAs). This accounts for the majority, over £6 billion, of its budget.

4.5   The Higher Education Funding Council for England (HEFCE) is responsible for distributing Government funding to universities and other higher education institutions. Research Councils and other Government bodies, including the Office of Science and Technology (OST) and the RDAs, also distribute funds to HE for research and innovation activity. In Scotland, the further and higher education funding functions have been merged together into the Scottish Further and Higher Education Funding Council. Funding has similarly been brought together in the Departmental frameworks of the Wales and Northern Ireland Governments.

Oversight 4.6   The implementation of the Skills Strategy in England is overseen by the Skills Alliance, a Ministerially led group consisting of Government departments, delivery agencies such as the LSC, HEFCE and Jobcentre Plus, and key external organisations such as the CBI, TUC, NIACE and the Associations of Learning Providers and Colleges. Employers are able to provide advice on the skills system through their participation in the Skills Alliance, through the Skills for Business Network (SSCs and SSDA) and on the employment system through the National Employment Panel (NEP) and its local employer coalitions.

Complexity 4.7   The Review has found that the complexity of the current system prevents employers and individuals from effectively investing in skills improvements. It has heard concerns from employers, trades unions and Government agencies within the skills system itself, about the complexity, duplication of responsibility and bureaucracy in the system. Richard Lambert, Director General of the CBI, said that the system should be 'substantially simplified'. He argues that this is a vital measure if employer engagement is to move beyond the 'bemused indifference' of today.

Employer 4.8   Most of the bodies tasked with delivering skills improvements have employer **involvement** representation or input. For example, at least 40 per cent of the LSC's national and local board members must have "substantial recent business or commercial experience".[1] Nonetheless, these roles for employers still tend to focus on involvement in planning and funding allocation decisions – trying to predict demand rather than ensuring the system is flexible enough to respond effectively as demand changes. In addition, employer representation has too often focused on carrying out of governance responsibilities rather than for delivering employer influence over strategic priorities. The fragmented nature of the skills system means that employer influence is often diluted across a wide array of bodies. Employers are baffled by the complex and often overlapping responsibilities of the bodies in the system.

---

[1] *The Learning and Skills Council Prospectus, Learning to succeed,* DfEE, 1999.

Recent progress

Demand-led system

4.9 Recent reforms have aimed to develop a more 'demand led' system, responding to demand rather than trying to plan supply. Train to Gain provides flexible training, designed to meet the needs of employers and employees. Providers only receive funding if they effectively meet the needs of their customers. The Employer Training Pilots show that this approach leads to provision that better reflects the needs of consumers increasing relevance, completion rates and therefore value for money.

Sector Skills Councils

4.10 A key point of employer involvement in the system is the network of Sector Skills Councils (SSCs) established across the UK from 2002. Their main tasks have been to drive up employer demand for skills and influence provision through drawing up Sector Skills Agreements (SSAs) to ensure that planned provision meets employer needs. They have also had a lead role in developing Sector Qualification Strategies, alongside QCA and developing Skills Academies, together with the LSC. The network of SSCs is showing promising signs of improving employer engagement. One half of all UK establishments are aware of the Skills for Business network, SSDA, SSCs or their own SSC and awareness is rising.[2] Employer awareness of their own SSC varies widely but is rising steadily and is highest in those SSCs that are longest established.

Building a fully demand led system

4.11 The Review has concluded that delivering a fully demand-led system is the only way to ensure that the UK achieves world class skills and that the skills delivered are economically valuable. To ensure this, the Review has developed recommendations focused on:

- **demand-led funding.** Routing public funding for adult vocational skills through demand-led routes, ending the supply-side planning of skills provision;

- **strengthening the employer voice.** Rationalising the number of bodies aiming to articulate the views of employers into a single Commission for Employment and Skills; and

- **economically valuable skills.** Reformed and relicensed Sector Skills Councils, with one of their functions focused on ensuring vocational qualifications reflect skills valued by employers.

DEMAND-LED FUNDING

4.12 As set out above, planning skills provision, no matter who does the planning, has always generated too much provision being 'supply driven' to meet plans and poorly articulated employer demand, rather than 'demand led' to meet employers' and individuals' needs. The LSC is acting to simplify the planning system, restructuring at regional and local levels, reducing the amount of detail it requires from colleges and providers. Significant progress has been made to lighten the regulatory burden, but more is needed to shift the LSC's role more decisively to funding and ensuring effective competition for post-19 vocational training.

4.13 However, history tell us supply-side planning of this sort cannot effectively meet the needs of employers, individuals and the economy. **The Review recommends a fully demand-led approach, with an end to this supply-side planning of provision.** While colleges and providers will still need to plan the types of provision they want to offer, including the broad vocational areas in which they wish to specialise, this planning should not be done by other bodies, including the LSC.

---

[2] *Skills for business network 2005: survey of employers*, SSDA, Research Report 18, 2005.

4.14 The Government has introduced reforms to make adult skills funding more demand-led. In England, flexible training for employees outside this framework of planning is provided through Train to Gain, currently being rolled out and discussed more fully in Box 4.1. Pilots of Learner Accounts, giving purchasing power to individuals, will begin at Level 3 soon. The recent Skills White Paper committed to extending this demand-led approach further so that the majority of funds would be distributed through these routes. Individual Learning Accounts operate in both Scotland and Wales and details of these schemes are included in Chapter 6. All these measures are still relatively small in the context of the overall adult skills budget – the vast majority of funding is currently planned at a very detailed level.

Box 4.1: Train to Gain

Employer Training Pilots (ETPs) were established in England in September 2002 to test a new approach to training of low-skilled employees. They had a 'core offer' which consisted of:

- free (or highly subsidised) training for employees to reach a basic skills or first, full Level 2 qualification;

- paid time in which employees could undertake the training;

- wage compensation to employers to help meet the cost of employee paid time off for training; and

- free information, advice and guidance for employees and employers.[a]

By the final year of the pilots, ETPs covered a total of 20 of the 47 local Learning and Skills Council (LSC) areas in England. By March 2006, a total of 30,000 employers and 250,000 employees had been involved in the pilots.

Evaluation shows that the most attractive element of ETPs to employers is the free and subsidised training. This was true of 'hard to reach' employers, but these also found the skills brokerage element of the pilots (whereby their skill needs were assessed and matched to suitable provision) relatively more attractive than other employers. Once all the learners who started have either left or completed training, success rates are likely to be around 70 per cent. However, there is evidence that the ETP pilots have been reaching those employers who were already engaged in developing the skills of their employees.[b]

In PBR 2004, the Government announced the rollout across England of Train to Gain, which broadly follows the ETP model. Unlike the pilots, Train to Gain is designed to offer support for employers in sourcing the full range of their training needs, while retaining a core of fully funded training up to first Level 2. Reforms include focusing brokers on employers less likely to engage in skills development in order to reduce deadweight. Around 60 per cent of employers engaged in the scheme were classified as 'hard-to-reach'.[c] Train to Gain will be up to full capacity by 2007-08, when it is forecast to deliver around 175,000 first, full Level 2 qualifications each year. Three Level 3 Train to Gain trials have also been launched, which will test the willingness of employers to contribute to the cost of training at Level 3.

---

[a] *Developing workforce skills: piloting a new approach*, HM Treasury, 2002.

[b] *Employer Training Pilots: Final Evaluation Report*, IES, 2006.

[c] Defined as not recognised as holding an Investors in People accreditation and no formally recorded training in the past 12 months.

4.15   The common feature of these programmes is that skills providers do not receive funding unless they attract learners. This puts employers and individuals far more in the driving seat than the current planned system. Rather than trying to recruit learners into planned courses that aim to anticipate demand, providers must design provision more flexibly to meet the needs of individuals and employers. This sort of provision is far more attractive to individuals and employers and so is far more likely to lead to increased training in the UK than attempts to plan provision on behalf of employers.

4.16   **The Review recommends that all publicly funded, adult vocational skills in England, apart from community learning and programmes for those with learning problems and disabilities, go through demand-led routes by 2010. This means all adult skills funding should be routed through Train to Gain and Learner Accounts by 2010.** This will give FE providers a real incentive to deliver the skills that employers and individuals need flexibly and responsively – if they do not, they will not receive public funding. This will ensure that providers deliver training that directly reflects demand from local employers and individuals. The Devolved Administrations should consider how best to ensure that provision is effectively led by the needs of employers and individuals.

The Learning and Skills Council   **4.17**   In England, the LSC, as discussed above, currently focuses on strategy, planning, contracting and funding for both adult skills and 16-19 provision. This includes funding for Apprenticeships and capital investment in FE Colleges. The 16-19 budget accounts for around two thirds of the LSC budget. **The switch to demand-led funding and end to the supply-side planning of adult skills provision fundamentally changes the role of planning bodies, such as the LSC, which will require a further significant streamlining.** Within this demand-led approach, there will remain four key elements of a national framework. First, the Government will identify priorities for investment of public funds. Second, the LSC will only fund programmes leading to qualifications approved by SSCs. Third, the LSC will work to ensure quality by identifying providers that can receive public funds – this process should ensure that all providers of good quality are accredited. Fourth, the LSC will act to promote effective competition.

4.18   The LSC has made good progress in streamlining its operations. Going forward, the Review recommends further significant streamlining of the LSC and its working relationships with other partners. In the truly demand-led system of 2010, the LSC should not undertake detailed planning at national, regional or local level. Rather, it should focus on processing funding for Train to Gain and Learner Accounts and ensuring effective competition. The LSC must be responsive to the needs of employers, but should not try to represent the 'voice of employers'. For good governance reasons, the LSC should feature strong employer representation. However, it is the Commission for Employment and Skills, described below, and SSCs that will be the voice of employers over employment and skills.

Demand led higher education   **4.19**   The principles of Train to Gain – delivering skills flexibly according to employer and individual demand – should apply to higher education too. Current Train to Gain pilots in the North West, North East and South West are already enabling brokers to provide information and advice to employers about higher level opportunities. **The Review recommends that a portion of higher education funding for vocational courses, currently administered through HEFCE in England, be delivered through a similar demand-led mechanism as Train to Gain. This should use Government funding to lever in greater investment by employers at Level 4 and Level 5.** This will change the incentives of HE providers to respond effectively to employer and individual demand as envisaged in the Higher Education White Paper in 2003.

4.20   The Higher Education White Paper stated that new higher education growth should not be *'more of the same'*, based on traditional three year honours degrees.[3] Rather, additional provision should be based on new types of programme offering specific, job-related skills such as Foundation degrees. The Review recommends that this is the right basis for future HE expansion, using Train to Gain and new types of employer led provision to progress both towards the 50 per cent participation target and to the broader adult attainment target. There should also be greater emphasis on level 5 activity, again in collaboration with employers.

A STRENGTHENED EMPLOYER VOICE

4.21   To deliver economically valuable skills, employers need a strong voice and must be able to scrutinise and shape strategy and delivery. At present, employers are asked to articulate their needs through a plethora of advisory and planning bodies scattered across the skills system. As a result, employers routinely complain that the system is too complex and they are unable to exercise effective influence over it.

Commission for Employment and Skills

Commission for Employment and Skills

4.22   Strengthen the employer voice, through the creation of a dynamic, employer-led Commission for Employment and Skills to deliver greater leadership and influence, within a national framework of individual rights and responsibilities. This will rationalise the existing system by merging and streamlining the Sector Skills Development Agency (SSDA) and the National Employment Panel (NEP), both operating across the UK, into a new organisation. In England, the Commission will also replace the Ministerially-led Skills Alliance and will ensure better integration of the current, disjointed Employment and Skills services. It will be responsible for:

- reporting on progress towards the UK's world class ambitions; scrutinising system objectives and delivery; recommending policy and operational improvements and innovations; and

- SSCs and a network of Employment and Skills Boards.

4.23   Establishing the employer-led Commission, will help to 'depoliticise' the skills agenda by securing a broad political and stakeholder consensus for the UK's world-class ambitions for 2020 and beyond. This will allow the UK to take a clearer, long term view of its employment and skills needs towards 2020. It should report to relevant senior Ministers in central Government and the devolved administrations. It will be chaired by an eminent business leader and comprise senior, high profile figures, including the Director General of the CBI and the General Secretary of the TUC. It will also include independent members, for example, relevant academics and representatives from the voluntary sector.

4.24   The Devolved Administrations in Scotland, Wales and Northern Ireland have responsibility for education and skills policy. Additional responsibilities in the Devolved Administrations will be subject to discussions and agreement with the Governments in each country.

---

[3] *The Future of Higher Education*, DfES, 2003.

Sector Skills Councils

4.25   Sector Skills Councils (SSCs) are beginning to effectively engage employers. Over three fifths of employers who have had dealings with their SSC think that SSCs have had a positive impact on skills development in their sector. Nearly two thirds of employers who deal with their SSC are satisfied. This includes those employers who operate across a number of SSCs with different business and occupational areas. The evaluation shows that there are significant variations by sector in performance.[4] Chart 4.2 shows employer satisfaction with the labour market information provided by their SSC.

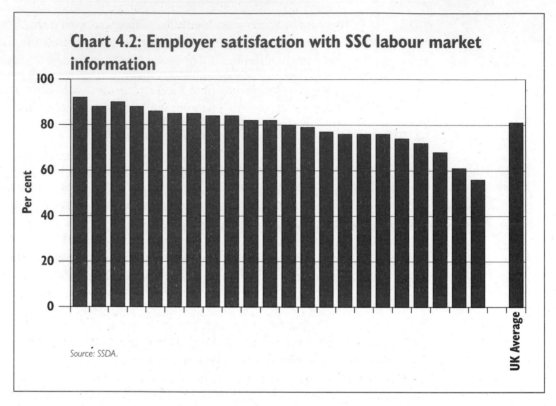

Chart 4.2: Employer satisfaction with SSC labour market information

Source: SSDA.

4.26   The experience of other countries, including the Netherlands and Australia, shows that a sectoral approach can work.[5] However, while there are some very successful SSCs, performance in the UK is patchy with some lacking effective engagement with key employers. The Review believes that this is a result of:

- **conflicting objectives.** SSCs are charged with engaging employers. But they are also meant to be self-financing by 2008, diverting activity from employer representation and preventing them in some cases from being an impartial 'voice of business';

- **lack of clear remit.** SSCs are charged with a lengthening list of responsibilities including negotiating Sector Skills Agreements with supply side partners, Sector Qualification Strategies, labour market information and a range of regional and national planning activities. This remit is stretched and too often tied to planning that cannot meet employer needs such as planning deals with the supply side through SSAs;

---

[4] *Skills for business network 2005: Survey of employers*, Research report 18, 2005.

[5] *Lessons From Abroad: Developing Sector Based Approaches to Skills*, Ashton and Sung, Sector Skills Development Agency, 2006.

- performance management. The current performance management regime is hampered by unclear accountabilities; and

- maturity and leadership. Even the oldest SSC is only four years old. The more long-standing SSCs tend to be among the strongest performing. The quality of leadership is absolutely crucial.

4.27   The Review recommends a new, clearer remit for SSCs, focused on:

- lead role in vocational qualifications. As detailed below, SSC's will be responsible for identifying and approving vocational qualifications for their sectors in England with only SSC-approved, vocational qualifications at NVQ Levels 1 to 5, including Foundation Degrees, eligible for public funding;

- lead role in collating and communicating sectoral labour market data. Each SSC should be responsible for ensuring up to date labour market information, which is consistent and comparable across sectors, and for communicating the occupational needs in their sectors;

- raising employer engagement, demand and investment. Drawing up Sector Skills Agreements among employers on the demand side that include hard attainment targets for employers to deliver improvements in skills, including through Apprenticeships and National Skills Academies. Chapter 5 discusses this in more detail; and

- considering collective measures. Considering whether there is support within a sector for introducing collective measures, such as a levy or licence to practise. Such measures should not be forced on a sector. As now, SSCs should introduce them if a clear majority of employers support them.

4.28   This clearer remit will make it easier to judge whether SSCs are performing effectively. The increased responsibilities SSCs will have under this remit, particularly their lead role in qualifications, will give employers a much greater incentive to engage with their SSC and performance manage it from the bottom up. The Commission will performance manage SSCs from the top down, relicensing those that are failing.

ENSURING QUALIFICATIONS REFLECT ECONOMICALLY VALUABLE SKILLS

4.29   Much of the publicly funded vocational system is focused on delivering qualifications. The Review's skills ambition is not solely focused on qualifications. As Chapter 2 set out in more detail, employers and individuals improve skills in a number of ways, all of which are important. Qualifications provide a useful international benchmark and are valued by employers and individuals as a proxy for skills.

4.30   Employers value the signals that qualifications provide about the abilities of individuals when they are recruiting staff. Qualifications form a major part of employer recruitment strategies. According to the Chartered Institute of Personnel and Development (CIPD), the contents of the application form or CV, including qualifications gained, are identified as the most frequently used selection method (66 per cent).[6] It is clear that qualifications provide important signals to employers as well as enabling portability for individuals in the labour market.

---

[6] CIPD Recruitment, Retention and Turnover Survey 2006.

4.31   The majority of individuals prefer studying towards a qualification[7] and over one half of employers feel it is quite or very important that the training provided leads to a qualification.[8] The most common reasons are to enable staff to do their jobs (24 per cent) and to motivate staff (14 per cent). Individuals are significantly more likely to be in work with every level of qualification gained. Around 90 per cent of those with a Level 4 or above qualification are in work, compared to less than 50 per cent of those with no qualifications.

4.32   However, qualifications only add economic value when they deliver skills that employers and individuals need. The higher wages that employers are prepared to pay to those with particular qualifications are a measure of the value employers attach to them and how closely they match the skills valued by employers. At present, too many qualifications, particularly at Level 2, have low or no wage returns, suggesting that they too often lack economic value. Some NVQ2's have no wage return, although they have a return of around 6 per cent when delivered in the workplace.[9] This compares to an average return of around 15 per cent for A Levels and 25 per cent for five GCSEs at grades A*-C.[10]

Complexity   **4.33**   It is well recognised that the English qualification system is overly complex. The Foster Review described the English system as *'confusing and complex with 115 Awarding Bodies and in excess of 5,000 qualifications in the National Qualifications Framework'* and noted that *'the qualifications system is not easy for learners, employers and others to understand or navigate'.*[11] According to a survey for QCA, ACCAC (Wales) and CCEA (Northern Ireland) in 2005, *'too many qualifications within the same sectors led to widespread confusion, reinforced by a lack of understanding of what the different levels of qualifications actually meant'.*[12] This report identified the number of qualifications in the UK as in excess of 22,636.

4.34   This complexity, combined with the low economic value delivered by some qualifications, has constrained investment in skills by employers and individuals – too often, neither can get the skills they want from the current qualification system. This has driven the low value historically attached to vocational qualifications in the UK relative to academic qualifications. The Review has found that the complexity of the qualifications system and low labour market value delivered by some qualifications result from key faults in the current system for developing qualifications. The next section sets out the Review's analysis of these faults and recommendations for addressing them.

The current approach

4.35   As with much of the education system, the qualification system varies across the nations of the UK, although there are many similarities, particularly in vocational qualifications. The system also differs greatly between the further and higher education sectors. Most qualifications in higher education, such as degrees and postgraduate qualifications are typically offered by institutions, rather than through intermediary awarding bodies as in FE. Chart 4.3 illustrates the different bodies that make up the vocational qualification system for NVQ 1 to 5 in England.

---

[7] National Adult Learning Survey, LSC, 2002.

[8] *The market for qualifications in the UK,* PWC, 2005.

[9] *An in-depth analysis of the returns to National Vocational Qualifications obtained at Level 2,* Dearden et al, CEE, 2004.

[10] See, for example, *Returns to education: A non-technical summary of CEE work and policy discussion,* Sianesi, Institute for Fiscal Studies and Centre for the Economics of Education, 2003.

[11] *Realising the potential: A review of the future role of further education colleges,* Andrew Foster, DfES, 2005.

[12] *The market for qualifications in the UK,* PWC, 2005.

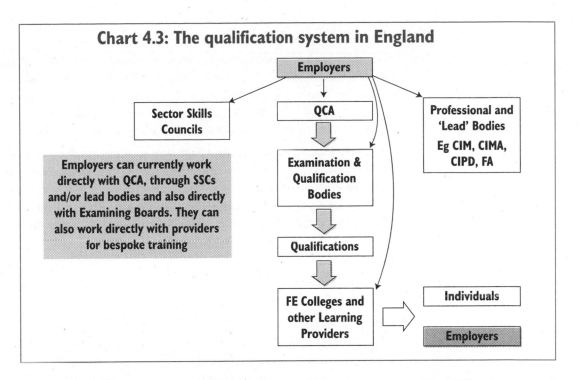

Chart 4.3: The qualification system in England

Developing qualifications

4.36 The process of developing a vocational qualification begins with the development of National Occupational Standards. These are the building blocks of qualifications, describing what people in a particular occupation need to be able to do to be competent. Occupational standards are currently drawn up by Sector Skills Councils. Awarding bodies then aim to design qualifications that will ensure those passing it have gained the skills outlined in the Standards. The QCA regulates awarding bodies, ensuring consistent standards across all provision. In turn the LSC mainly funds qualifications that are QCA approved. The delivery of qualifications is managed by a combination of providers, awarding bodies and the LSC.

4.37 It is right that employers, through SSCs, draw up National Occupational Standards – they are best placed to describe the competencies needed in a particular occupation. However, representations to the Review have highlighted the complexity and drawn-out nature of the resulting process of turning these standards into qualifications. The large number of bodies involved in qualification design makes it difficult for employers to effectively influence the process. Consequently, employers are distanced from the process of designing qualifications and too often feel that the end product does not adequately reflect the National Occupational Standards. As a result, too many qualifications lack value in the labour market.

Higher Education

4.38 The picture at the higher end is different. NVQ Levels 4 and 5 are developed in the same way as other vocational qualifications. However, there are key differences in the way that other higher education qualifications, including Foundation Degrees, are developed. Universities are responsible for developing and delivering their own courses. Institutions, rather than exam bodies, award degrees, including Foundation Degrees, and postgraduate qualifications. Therefore to influence content, employers and their SSCs have to develop direct relationships with universities.

4.39 There are many good examples of employer and higher education collaboration, often prompted by SSCs. Skillset, the SSC for the audio-visual industries, with the backing of major employers such as BBC and ITV, are establishing 'Skillset Academies' based within HE institutions. E-Skills, the SSC for the IT and telecommunications sector, is helping to deliver a new degree – Information Technology Management for Business – in a number of UK universities with support from employers such as IBM, Microsoft and BT.

Box 4.1: What happens in other countries?

Other examination and qualification systems are simpler than in England or the UK. In many countries, institutions award qualifications at FE level rather than awarding bodies – similar to the HE position in the UK. The US community college system and the Australian Technical and Further Education (TAFE) system demonstrate this approach, as well as a generally more fluid relationship with HE level provision in the respective countries.

The Australian system, shown in the chart below, relies on the autonomy of a series of large TAFE providers. These and other providers (including employers directly) are licensed at the state level to provide programmes (content is directly agreed with ITABs, the Australian equivalent of SSCs) leading to institutionally certified courses. There is no equivalent of the QCA, of examining boards/bodies or the LSC. Funds are distributed directly from the Commonwealth and State Governments.

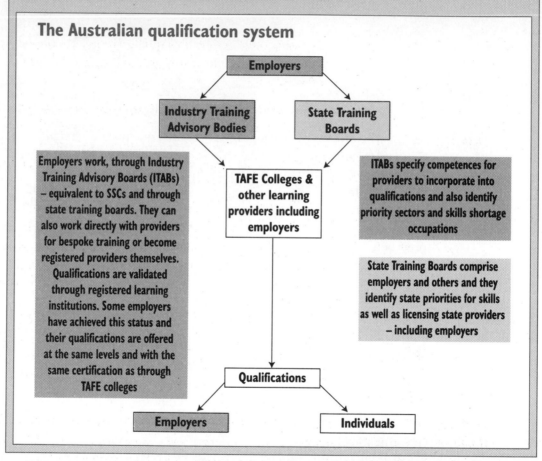

The Australian qualification system

THE REVIEW'S PROPOSALS: EMPLOYER-DRIVEN VOCATIONAL QUALIFICATIONS

4.40   The Review's analysis finds that the process of developing vocational qualifications from National Occupational Standards is drawn out and overly complex. This limits the ability of employers to effectively influence the process. It is this complexity, combined with a lack of effective employer influence, which has led to the proliferation of qualifications, too many of which are not valued in the labour market. The Review has developed recommendations to simplify the process of developing qualifications, putting employers more in control, so that qualifications better reflect economically valuable skills. The Government and Devolved Administrations have established a four country UK Programme board to establish a rationalised, unit and credit based set of arrangements, based on employer and labour market needs. The Review has developed recommendations to assist this by simplifying the process of developing qualifications, putting employers in control, so that qualifications better reflect economically valuable skills.

4.41 The Review recommends that Sector Skills Councils continue to lead in developing National Occupational Standards, the building blocks of qualifications. It recommends that SSCs are also placed in charge of a simplified process of approving qualifications that follows this. In practice, this means:

- Sector Skills Councils should be responsible for approving qualifications after their development by awarding boards or other organisations. They should reject qualifications if they fail to adequately capture the competences laid down in occupational standards. The QCA in England will continue to maintain the national regulatory framework with consistency and comparability of standards across sectors and levels;

- SSCs will be able to approve qualifications developed by an organisation, including education institutions and employers, if these meet the required standards; and

- for vocational qualifications, only those approved by SSCs should qualify for public funding. This would apply to funding for work-based learning qualifications such as NVQs, including Levels 4 and 5, through the LSC in England. SSCs should develop a short list of such qualifications, with a very significant reduction in the overall number, by 2008. Arrangements in Wales, Scotland and Northern Ireland should be developed by the Devolved Administrations.

4.42 In this way, only qualifications valued and approved by employers will attract public funding. The Commission will be responsible for performance managing the SSCs to make sure they perform this role effectively and that they collaborate appropriately together and with other bodies such as QCA over generic skills and competences. Ensuring that only those qualifications approved by employers attract public funding will lead to a simplified qualification system, with fewer qualifications overall and only qualifications delivering economically valuable skills, attracting a return in the labour market, attracting public funding. SSCs should be specifically charged with significantly reducing the number of qualifications.

Accrediting employer training **4.43** A further important aspect of this reformed system will be to allow SSCs to approve new qualifications based on employers' own internal training where this meets national quality assurance requirements. This includes higher level provision offered by employers, where it is of a sufficiently high standard. This means that individual employers will be able to offer their own, nationally recognised qualifications, where their training has clear economic value.

4.44 If the training requires extra knowledge or competence in order to qualify for full accreditation, then this should be accessed through brokers and the relevant funding body. Incentives to develop this employer role should exist through LSC and HEFCE demand led funding streams both for employers and for institutions such as FE colleges and universities. When employers and providers are allowed to accredit training, they will be subject to the same ongoing quality assurance procedures as other qualifications.

4.45 Similarly, colleges and other providers should be able to offer their own qualifications, subject to SSC approval and consistency with a national regulatory framework. This will happen where such qualifications are of clear economic value, demonstrably relevant to employers and fill a clear gap in the market. Awarding Bodies have immense experience of the development of qualifications and should support SSCs, employers and providers. SSCs in their enhanced role, will have responsibility for approving vocational qualifications in their sectors. The QCA will continue to have a vital regulatory role in England but should adopt a transparent, more risk-based, 'arm's length' approach such as that shown in other sectors such as the Financial Services Authority.

Further Education **4.46**   Building on the recommendations of the Foster Review and the subsequent DFES White Paper,[13] the Review's recommendations will have a significant impact on Further Education colleges and providers. The strengthened focus on skills and employability, alongside a more responsive system for employers and a more demand led funding system, has provided strong incentives for colleges and other providers to focus on the needs of employers and individuals. Incentives for greater employer involvement in FE include the need for greater specialisation by colleges. Further development of Centres of Vocational Excellence (CoVEs) and the new Employer Standard will combine with Train to Gain and the ability of colleges to offer qualifications to form a vastly improved offer to employers.

4.47   FE colleges and providers will be vital to all of the ambitions described in Chapters 2 and 3. Their role in delivering basic and intermediate skills is already significant and enhanced ambitions will require even more support from the sector at these levels. New ambitions for the amount and type of higher level skills will also depend, in part, on the FE sector, with a greater role in delivering employer facing learning at Levels 4 and 5, including Foundation degrees. This too will help colleges to further develop their offer to employers by offering courses across every level of learning.

4.48   The Review's recommendations to enable providers to offer their own qualifications, with the support of SSCs, also builds on the proposal in the recent FE Bill to allow colleges to offer Foundation Degrees. Together with greater levels of demand-led funding, the Review's recommendations represent a further incentive for closer working with employers. Significantly, it will enable a more direct and productive relationship between FE colleges, providers and employers with greater institutional autonomy and the potential for improved 'business to business' collaboration.

CONCLUSION

4.49   This chapter has described the reforms recommended by the Review to build a more industry led skills and qualification system that delivers what employers and individuals need within a national framework. At the heart of this is a reformation of Sector Skills Councils so that they can fully articulate the views of employers. They will be given new responsibility for developing vocational qualifications as part of a sharper, clearer remit.

4.50   Giving SSCs this clearer remit will enable their performance to be more clearly evaluated. Ensuring they have real responsibility will increase the incentives of employers to be more involved in their SSC. Finally, the new Commission for Employment and Skills will actively performance manage SSCs, withdrawing or varying the licences of those that are not up to scratch.

---

[13] *Getting on in business, getting on at work*, DFES, 2005.

4.51 These reforms to improve the role of industry in the skills system must be matched by dramatic simplification and an end to the micro planning of skills provision – creating a truly demand led system. To deliver this, the Review has recommended that adult skills funding in England be routed primarily through Train To Gain and Learner Accounts by 2010. This shift in responsibilities to SSCs and the CES, coupled with an end to micro planning has significant implications for other bodies, such as the LSC, in the skills system.

4.57 The outcome of these reforms will be a simplified, industry led system that depends on demand rather than central planning. This will transform the incentives of providers, requiring them to actively react to demand, rather than recruiting to fill supply. In turn, this will encourage greater investment in skills by employers and individuals.

4.58 In return for giving more control to employers, businesses have a responsibility for greater involvement, support and increasing investment. The following chapters set out the relative roles of employers and individuals in taking up opportunities to improve skills and proposals to increase their investment.

5

EMPLOYER ENGAGEMENT IN SKILLS

Chapter summary

Employers must play their part in achieving a world class skills base in the UK, raising their engagement in skills at all levels and using skills effectively. This chapter sets out the Review's recommendation for the Government and employers to work together to increase the skill levels of their workforce and ensure the effective use of skills in the workplace.

Employers will increase their engagement in skills if the skills delivery system meets their needs. Chapter 4 set out recommendations to give employers greater strategic control of the skills delivery and vocational qualification systems. To ensure that these meet the needs of the economy, employers must exercise this power. UK employers spend £33 billion a year on training. However, one third of employers do little or no training at all. A number of barriers, including awareness and the time and cost of training, constrain employer investment in and use of skills. These barriers impact in different ways in different types of firms and sectors. Evidence shows that in some parts of the economy, relatively poor management and leadership can affect both the demand for skills and whether they are used effectively in the workplace.

The Review recommends shared national action from the Government and employers. This will be a 'something for something' deal that ties rights to responsibilities, coupling increased and improved Government effort with increased and improved action by employers. This will deliver:

- **effective use of skills.** Skills must be effectively used for their benefits to be fully realised. The Review recommends the Government ensure appropriate provision of advice and brokerage services to help businesses to invest effectively in skills, and targeted support to improve management skills to ensure maximum use of skills in the workplace;

- **a labour force with a platform of skills.** The Review recommends Government commitment and funding to ensure the whole labour force has the platform of skills needed for work, but a responsibility for employers to help employees to gain these skills, including a legal entitlement to workplace training, if progress falls short, in 2010;

- **world class intermediate skills.** The Review recommends matched funding and employer powers to shape Apprenticeships, in return for hard edged attainment targets in SSAs to increase employer engagement that includes expanding the number of Apprentices in the UK to 500,000 a year by 2020; and

- **improved high skills.** The Review recommends changes to Government targets and funding to facilitate greater collaboration between employers and universities, in return for hard-edged commitments by employers to increase their investment in high skills.

5.1 Previous chapters set out the Review's recommendation that the UK aim to be a world leader in skills and the huge benefits this will bring. Employers will share in these benefits, but to ensure they are fully realised, firms must raise their demand for, and investment in, skills and effectively use skills in the workplace. This chapter sets out recommendations for shared action from the Government and employers, a 'something for something' approach that ties greater rights to increased responsibility.

THE ROLE OF EMPLOYERS

5.2   Chapter 2 set out the scale of the challenge faced by the UK if it is to achieve a world-class skills profile and respond effectively to globalisation. More than 70 per cent of the 2020 working age population have already left compulsory education and many of these are in work. The UK cannot rely solely on improving the skills of young people to deliver a world-class skills base in 2020 – those already in the labour market must have the opportunity to improve their skills as the global economy restructures.

5.3   As Chapter 1 showed, achieving a world class skills base will drive increased productivity and profitability for employers and improved public services. As global economic change continues, the skills of their employees will be the key way for employers to remain competitive in the global economy and to adapt to change. For both these reasons – the need for employees to improve their skills and the importance of skills for employers to be competitive – the Review argues that part of the drive to world class skills must be a shared national mission, with a 'something for something' deal between the Government and employers, tying rights to responsibilities.

Employment in   **5.4**   The UK economy has changed significantly over time. The service sector now **the UK** accounts for around three quarters of the UK economy. Almost 29 million people are employed in the UK. The largest industry by employment is the wholesale and retail sector. In 2006, 5.8 million people were employed in the public sector, 20 per cent of the workforce. Small firms with less than 50 employees account for around one quarter of employment, with large firms accounting for more than one half.

5.5   The challenges faced by each sector and size of firm differs, as do their skills needs and relative productivity. Both the public and private sectors, large firms and small, services and manufacturing, will face increased skills needs over the coming years. Each must play their part in raising their game.

Current employer   **5.6**   Employers already provide a substantial amount of training for their employees, as **investment in** set out in Chapter 2. However, most is unaccredited, training is disproportionately focused on **skills** the high skilled, and around one third of firms do no training at all. There are a number of barriers to efficient investment in skills. Lack of awareness of the benefits of training, the cost and time for training and the quality of leadership and management all constrain the scale and effectiveness of employer training in the UK.

A shared mission with employers

5.7   Chapter 4 set out reforms to the system for delivery of skills to simplify the system and place employers at its heart. Funding will no longer be planned but will be demand-led. There will be a single organisation, a Commission for Employment and Skills, uniting the employer voice and influence. Sector Skills Councils (SSCs) will significantly reduce the number of qualifications available, ensure they are economically valuable and provide the long-term labour market information that employers need to make informed decisions.

Shared action to   **5.8**   These reforms give employers and trades unions the power to ensure the skills and **meet world class** qualification systems deliver what they need and to ensure that valuable employer training is properly accredited. Employers need to exercise this power. They also need to increase their investment in portable, accredited training, particularly for low skilled employees. The Review recommends that employers work in partnership with the Government to deliver this increased investment, as part of a shared commitment to making the UK a world leader in skills.

5.9   This shared commitment will couple increased Government action at each skill level with specific employer commitments for greater investment in and use of skills at each level. Through this shared commitment, the UK can improve its productivity and businesses can more effectively compete in the global economy.

5.10   The Review recommends additional Government action tied to specific employer commitments at each skill level to ensure:

- **effective use of skills.** The Review recommends additional support and advice to ensure businesses can effectively invest in and use skills. Tied to this, employers have a responsibility to use these services, improving the quality of their leadership and management;

- **a labour force with a platform of skills.** The Review recommends the Government commit to funding and delivering training in a flexible way that meets the needs of employers. In return, employers must commit to enabling their employees to access work-based skills development, through a new legal entitlement to Train to Gain in England if the UK is falling short;

- **world-class intermediate skills.** Employers to make specific commitments to increase their attainment of intermediate skills, including through Sector Skills Agreements, leading to increasing the number of Apprentices in the UK to 500,000 a year by 2020; and

- **world-class high skills.** Widening the target to improve high skills so it focuses on workforce development and providing additional incentives for employers to invest. In return, employers to commit to greater attainment of high skills, including through hard targets for achievement in SSAs.

5.11   The following sections spell out in more detail what each of these commitments means in practice for employers and the Government.

EFFECTIVE USE OF SKILLS

5.12   The UK will not reap the benefits from a world class skills base set out in Chapter 2 unless the skills delivered are the ones employers and individuals need and businesses want, and know how to use effectively in the workplace. Similarly, employers will not invest further in skills unless they can see the benefits that such investment will bring and how they might use new skills.

Management and leadership

5.13   Good management is a prerequisite to improving business performance, a key aspect of which is effective use of workforce skills. It is managers in a business that decide on product and service strategies, whether to invest in training and how to deploy the skills of their workers. Improving management skills in the UK has two important effects; it increases the demand for skills and their effective deployment in the workplace, and it improves the overall standards of performance in organisations.

The UK has problems with management   **5.14**   While there are examples of very good management, the UK has some serious problems with management and leadership. Recent work found that the quality of management practice in manufacturing varied widely within countries and sectors, and overall the UK was ranked behind the USA, Germany and France.[1] A greater proportion of

---

[1] *Management practices across firms and nations*, Bloom, Dorgan, Dowdy, Van Reenan, Rippin, LSE-Mckinsey, 2005.

those classified as 'managers' by the Labour Force Survey hold low-level qualifications than in other 'higher' level occupations, such as professional occupations. For example, 41 per cent of managers hold less than a Level 2 qualification. This varies significantly across sectors and between firms.

Current measures to improve management

5.15 Employers invest a great deal in improving management. The provision of management training is only part of the solution. The Review's interim report showed that employers were up to five times more likely to provide training for managers or other senior staff than to those with low or no qualifications. However, a recent study showed that the UK spent €1,600 per manager on management development, less than any other country in Europe and compared to €4,400 in Germany.[2]

5.16 Improving management and leadership is already a key objective for business. The CBI describes it as one of their most important priorities, with just over one half of their employers believing that it is the most significant factor contributing to competitiveness.[3] The Small Business Service (SBS) also sees management and leadership as vital, stating that *'leadership and management capability is a key determinant of business success'*.[4]

5.17 The Government has introduced measures to help employers improve the quality of management and leadership in the UK. This has included measures within the Skills Strategy, the formation of the Commission for Excellence in Management and Leadership, funding for related training in small businesses and for Investors in People attainment and the ongoing work of the Leadership and Management Advisory Panel.

5.18 In the Skills Strategy, DfES allocated £43.7 million for a Leadership and Management programme, offering managers of organisations with between 20 and 250 employees up to £1,000 financial support to develop leadership and management skills. This has been largely brokered alongside the Train to Gain programme. Nearly 18,000 managers had their needs assessed and nearly 17,000 had agreed a Personal Development Plan by the end of March 2006.[5] The SBS found that, for every £1,000 of financial support grants given to small businesses through the Leadership and Management Programme operated by the LSC, an average additional investment of over £2,000 has been triggered.[6] 35,000 organisations are recognised by Investors in People and a further 23,000 organisations are working towards recognition, demonstrating a commitment to effective management practices.

The Review's proposals

5.19 The UK needs world class management skills to deliver the benefits of world class skills. Improving management and leadership is a complex and a challenging problem. Training will only make a contribution to tackling this problem if management training meets the needs of employers. To ensure this, the Review recommends that the Leadership and Management Advisory Panel advise the Commission for Employment and Skills on developing National Occupational Standards for management with the Management Standards Centre and building on work already done by the Chartered Management Institute. The Panel must work closely with SSCs so that key management qualifications are identified as part of Sector Qualification Strategies.

5.20 The Review has developed recommendations to increase employer investment in management skills. As discussed above, the Leadership and Management programme has

---

[2] *Leadership and management in the UK: Raising our ambition*, The Leadership and Management Advisory Panel, Submission to the Leitch Review, October 2006.

[3] *The Importance of Leadership and Management Skills to Employers – CBI Survey evidence*, CBI 2006.

[4] *Small Business Service proposals for the 2006 Pre Budget Report*, Small Business Service, 2006.

[5] *Leadership and management in the UK: Raising our ambition*, The Leadership and Management Advisory Panel, Submission to the Leitch Review, October 2006.

[6] *Small Business Service proposals for the 2006 Pre Budget Report*, Small Business Service, 2006.

successfully supported management development for firms with between 20 and 250 employees and has levered in significant private investment. **The Review recommends that it be extended to firms with between 10 and 20 employees, so that smaller firms are able to access its help and grow.**

5.21 Employer engagement with HE and commitment to continuous professional development can also help to drive up the quality of management. The growth in UK business school provision shows that employers and universities can successfully work together. The Review's recommendation that the focus of HE be expanded to focus on workforce development will facilitate this, as will the recommendation that funding be demand-led, detailed in Chapter 4.

Awareness, information and advice

5.22 For employers to invest effectively in high performance working and skills development, they need not only good management and leadership, but also effective information and advice. Employers need accurate information on the state of the labour market and developments in the economy. The system for improving skills must be simple, flexible and transparent, as set out in Chapter 4. More must be done to ensure high quality advice for all employers to enable them to find appropriate training to meet their needs.

Labour market **5.23** Labour market information (LMI) provides a context in which a firm makes an **information** investment decision. At present, there are various sources of labour market information for employers. However there is little coordination between different sources, meaning that in some instances they deliver contradictory information. As Chapter 4 set out, effective LMI is an essential tool for SSCs to fulfil their role. **The Review recommends that SSCs have primary responsibility for gathering and disseminating LMI, within a common framework.**

Advising **5.24** Once an employer has the LMI that gives them a context for their decisions, they must **employers** decide how to invest to improve their business. At the firm level, skills brokers can raise awareness, help firms to diagnose their skill needs and signpost them to appropriate providers. This must be set in the context of improving a business. Where brokerage has worked well, it has repeatedly been reported to be the most effective part of the Train to Gain package after the free training.[7]

5.25 A wide range of Government bodies aim to support businesses. The main service in England is Business Link, which is managed by the Regional Development Agencies to provide business support services, mainly to small firms. In some regions, it also provides the brokerage for Train to Gain.

5.26 In addition, there are multiple trade associations, local and regional groups of employers and supply chain projects, all of which are working to improve productivity and efficiency, including through promoting skills development.

5.27 This system is complex and employers often find it difficult to know where they should go to for help. Responsibility for managing business support has been transferred to the RDAs, and the Government has launched a review of business support services. **It is vital that current business support is simplified and strengthened. Skills advice must be integrated as part of this wider system of support. Train to Gain brokers, managed by the RDAs and LSC, will be the key skills advice arm of this business support.** As Box 4.1 set out, there is some evidence that in the Employer Training Pilots, brokers focused on employers already likely to engage with skills development. As the overall volume of training increases,

---

[7] *Employer Training Pilots: final evaluation report*, DfES, 2006.

the Review supports the drive to focus brokers on engaging with 'harder to reach' employers and employees. In this way, the deadweight found in the pilots can be reduced.

5.28   It is vital that larger employers are fully engaged, aware of skill needs and able to source appropriate training if the UK is to meet longer-term ambitions. For larger firms, the LSC funds a National Employer Service (NES). This provides large firms with a single point of contact with the LSC. **As Train To Gain continues to roll out, the NES should be reformed, expanded and re-energised so that it provides a credible, professional advisory service for large employers.**

5.29   Jobcentre Plus also has a National Account Management Service (NAMS). This provides firms with a significant number of vacancies a full recruitment service and individual Account Manager. Chapter 7 sets out the case for better integrating skills and employment services for individuals. There is a clear case for doing the same for large employers, integrating recruitment services with training advice. **The Commission should make recommendations on how to ensure the NES and NAMS work in an integrated way.**

Advising employees   **5.30**   Motivating employees to learn is critical to ensuring training is effectively used in the workplace. Employees need information and advice so that they can also recognise their own skills needs and know what training and development opportunities are available. Trades Unions are increasingly involved in the skills agenda and are playing a key role in engaging both adults and employers, especially in workplaces where learning opportunities may have been limited in the past. The Union Learning Fund, established in 1998, has been highly effective together with the growing network of Union Learning Representatives (ULRs) in workplaces throughout the UK and the launch of 'unionlearn' earlier this year. There are now more than 15,000 trained ULRs in workplaces with a target of 22,000 for 2010.

A LABOUR FORCE WITH A PLATFORM OF SKILLS

5.31   Earlier chapters set out the UK's deficit in basic and low skills, with 5 million adults lacking functional literacy and 7 million lacking functional numeracy. Increasingly, Level 2 is the minimum platform of skills required for employment and business competitiveness. Of the 11.5 million adults currently lacking a Level 2 qualifications, almost 7 million are in work. Around one half of those lacking functional literacy and numeracy skills are in work. Achieving a world class proportion of people with a platform of skills will require the commitment and sustained action from the Government, employers, trades unions and individuals.

The current situation

5.32   The Review has found that the barriers employers face in training particularly constrain employer investment in training low skilled workers. For example, businesses may find it difficult to value the indirect benefits of training at lower levels, such as reductions in staff turnover and improvements in morale and motivation, all of which also contribute to efficiency. Firms may fear that generic training at lower levels could lead to other firms poaching their workers.

5.33   Employer concerns over the relevance of qualifications are particularly acute at the lower level. As Chapter 4 showed, many Level 2 courses have little or no wage return. Employers also see basic skills, such as literacy and numeracy, as being the responsibility of the school system and the Government, with businesses more responsible for training beyond this. Rather than investing in the basic and foundation skills of their employees, they find ways to work around employee skill needs in the workplace.

The current approach 5.34   The most recent and successful approach to delivering this platform of skills to employees in England is Train to Gain, based on the Employer Training Pilots (ETPs), delivering training flexibly and tailored to meet the needs of employers and employees. Train to Gain is a clear success and was summarised in Box 2.1. The Government has committed to increase funding for Train to Gain to £1 billion by 2010. The Devolved Administrations have their own approach. For example, in Wales the Management Development Programme offers matched funding for bespoke training.

5.35   The experience of the ETPs suggests that most large employers and a substantial number of smaller firms will engage with the programme. By the end of the three years of the pilots, more than 70 per cent of large firms in pilot areas had engaged. Ensuring that the capacity of the programme can meet this initial high demand will be a challenge. Beyond this, there is a risk that demand will fall short of that required to meet the Review's ambition.

5.36   It will be a significant challenge for the UK to move from 69 per cent of the adult population qualified to Level 2 in 2005 to exceeding 90 per cent by 2020, achieving the world class projection of 95 per cent as soon as is feasible. Through the development of Train to Gain and the National Employer Service, the Government needs to ensure that employers of all sizes and types can get support while still ensuring that Government funds are used to leverage additional investment in training.

Going further

5.37   The move from 69 per cent of the adult population qualified to at least Level 2 in 2005 to exceeding 90 per cent by 2020 and achieving 95 per cent as soon as is feasible will be stretching and difficult to achieve. There is a risk that the UK will not move onto the trajectory required. The Review has developed recommendations to fill this gap, should it arise.

Additional voluntary action by employers 5.38   Many employers in England are already engaging in Train to Gain and in training their low-skilled employees, because they recognise the long term benefits from providing this training, and the value in taking up the Government's offer of free training that is flexibly delivered. However, more needs to be done to ensure that as many low-skilled employees as possible are able to benefit.

5.39   In Wales, a Basic Skills Pledge enables employers to commit to ensuring all their employees are able to improve their basic skills. The Welsh Assembly Government has set a target of 50 per cent of employees being covered by 2010 and the pledge already covers 10 per cent of employees. **The Review recommends that the Government work with employer representative organisations to support and encourage all employers in the UK in making a skills pledge, building on recent experience in Wales. The skills pledge would be a specific promise to the workforce that every eligible employee would be helped to gain basic skills and a Level 2 qualification. A major campaign would encourage all employers in the UK to make a skills pledge that every employee be enabled to gain basic skills and a first full Level 2 qualification – with funding from the Government, support from the Train to Gain brokerage service and time allowances at work.** The Review expects public sector organisations and partners to lead the way in committing to the pledge.

5.40   Employers could also go further, setting out plans to move their workforce to even higher skill levels and publicising their progress towards fulfilling their pledge. Collective Learning Funds, currently being developed by the DfES and the TUC, would encourage joint employer-union initiatives to increase the scope of training and development opportunities for their workforce and to commit new investment to this. In addition, these funds could encourage employees to co-invest their time along with the employer in a wider range of non job-specific training and development. Together with Workplace Learning Committees and

Learning Agreements, where appropriate, these could also form a key part of any employer commitment to the pledge. They have been particularly emphasised as effective routes to improve training activity by employer organisations such as the Engineering Employers Federation (EEF) and the CIPD.[8]

5.41   Investors in People can engage employers in developing the skills of their employees to enhance business performance, recognising achievement through a common standard. **The Government should, in consultation with the Commission and leading employers, review the remit of Investors in People, to consider how IiP UK and its products, including the Standard itself and the new 'Profile' tool, should be reshaped to support delivery of the Review's ambition.**

5.42   This initiative will need high profile 'champions'. If enough employers make this pledge, this could make a major contribution to the UK's skills position. Large employers, both public and private sector, account for over 50 per cent of employment and over 40 per cent of all low-skilled employees. The Government should lead by example in making the pledge on behalf of the public sector. Raising investment by employers in skills at all levels is a key responsibility for Sector Skills Councils and skills brokers, as set out in Chapter 4. They will do this through a range of awareness raising and engagement strategies. One mechanism for articulating employer commitments to increasing skills will be drawing up Sector Skills Agreements (SSAs). As Chapter 4 set out, these should have firm commitments from employers about how much they will raise attainment of skills.

5.43   Such voluntary action should help to move the UK toward the world-class ambition. However, there remains a strong risk that voluntary action is not sufficient to deliver the rate of change required. Both the Government and the Commission should judge whether the UK is on course for world-class skills. As set out in Chapter 3, the indicator for this should be the volume of people gaining skills, rather than the level of investment.

The role of compulsory mechanisms   **5.44**   The Review has considered a range of mechanisms that could be introduced if the Government and the Commission judge that the UK is not on track to meet its ambition of a world class proportion of adults qualified to at least Level 2. Compulsory mechanisms to ensure training for low-skilled employees, including licences to practise, training levies on employers and rights to time off, have been introduced in a number of other countries and in the UK in the past. The Review has found that these have had varying impact and success. The remaining Industrial Training Boards, the new training levy for the film industry and the increasing range of licences to practise show the beneficial impact that can be achieved. Only where employers are engaged and can access relevant training, and where individuals are motivated, can such measures increase training and productivity significantly. Box 5.1 sets out evidence on the impact of some of these options.

---

[8] *Employer Guide to Union Learning Representatives*, EEF Website, 2006; *Trade Union Learning Representatives*, CIPD Change Agenda Series, CIPD, 2004.

Box 5.1: International experience of compulsory training at work

A range of countries has introduced forms of compulsion to increase training of employees. The evidence shows that these work only where the training benefits employers, individuals are motivated to improve their skills and the schemes are carefully designed to be flexible.

One of the most common forms of compulsion is the right to time off for training. International evidence suggests that take up rates for rights to time off are higher if there are stronger incentives for employers to take an interest in the training. In the UK, the "time off for study or training" scheme for 16 or 17 year olds has an estimated take up of only 3 per cent. In Austria, a government financed leave scheme for employees of more than 3 years has a take up of only 0.1 per cent of the workforce, but funding is for training of more than 16 hours per week, taking employees out of work for long periods of time, and only employees who have been with the same employer for more than 3 years are eligible. However, in Denmark, time off for employees has an estimated annual take up rate of 9 per cent of the eligible population. The higher take up in Denmark is the result of improved incentives for both employers and employees to get involved – the training is financed by sectoral levies, targeted on low-skilled employees who have been with the same employer for more than 6 months and wage reimbursement is paid to individuals.[a]

Levies, which require firms to spend more on training, are another common form of compulsion. Levies can significantly increase the volume of training. For example, Tan estimated that the Malaysian levy increased the number of firms providing training by 20 per cent,[b] and Mehaut shows that expenditure on training in France rose significantly after the levy was introduced.[c]

A one size fits all approach does not always lead to subsequent increases in productivity. Noble found that the Australian levy produced a 23 per cent increase in training expenditure but there was little increase in productivity.[d] In practice, levies are often most effective in improving productivity in sectors where poaching of skills workers is a risk or highly sub-contracted industries such as construction. In 2003, 69 per cent of employers in the UK construction industry were in favour of retaining the levy system for their sector.

The key lesson from the international evidence and the UK's past experience is that compelling employers to train will only work if the training is delivered flexibly so it benefits the employer and coupled with action to engage employees.

[a] *Promoting adult learning*, OECD, 2005.

[b] *Do training levies work? Malaysia's HRDF and its Effects on Training and Firm-Level Productivity*, Tan, Working Paper, World Bank Institute, 2001.

[c] *Reforming the training system in France*, Mehaut, Industrial Relations Journal 36:4, 303-317, 2005.

[d] *International comparisons of Training Policies*, Noble, Human Resource Management Journal, Volume 7, Number 1, 1997.

5.45 The Review has concluded that, if voluntary action does not meet the scale needed, the UK should only go further if the training can be delivered in an employer-focused way that delivers demonstrable improvements in productivity – a blunt 'one size fits all' form of compulsion is unlikely to be effective.

5.46 In England, Train to Gain is an effective mechanism for achieving productive training and engaging both individuals and their employers. The Review has concluded that increasing the take up and scope of Train to Gain is the most appropriate way to ensure everyone can build the base of skills they need in the modern labour market. There is a real risk that, even with additional voluntary action, the UK will not reach the trajectory it needs to deliver this ambition.

Entitlement to workplace training

5.47 In 2010, the Government and the Commission should review progress in the light of take-up and employer delivery on their pledges. If the improvement rate is insufficient, the Review recommends that the Government introduce an individual legal entitlement to workplace training for employees lacking a Level 2 qualification or equivalent through Train to Gain in England, in consultation with employers and trades unions. This will allow time for further voluntary effort, but ensure that action is in place if this effort is not sufficient.

5.48 The legal entitlement to workplace training should be delivered through Train to Gain in England. This will mean that employers are able to design the content and delivery of the training to meet their needs. In this way, it will maximise the productivity benefits of training to the firm. By providing free training, delivering training both in and out of work time, and with the Government considering the appropriate role of wage compensation for small firms, it will also minimise the cost to the firm while training is underway.

5.49 An individual employee will be able to access their entitlement in a number of ways. They will hear about it through advertising, colleagues, employer, trades union (particularly union learning representatives), or their network of friends and family. They will either approach their line manager or the new careers service. If their employer does not have an existing relationship with the Train to Gain broker, the careers service or line manager would call the broker. With the agreement of the employer, employees should also be able to access this entitlement through time off, if more convenient.

5.50 The broker would conduct a skills assessment of the business, including identifying the most appropriate qualifications for the individual employees and a local training provider. The training provider would give a service that fitted with the needs of the firm and the individual, in terms of time commitment and timescale. On average, a Level 2 takes 75 hours of work time over an 8 month period, with another 25 hours from the individual's free time.

5.51 The entitlement will need to be carefully designed so that it minimises bureaucracy and avoids being overly prescriptive. It must be designed in consultation with employers and trades unions. It is likely that the entitlement will require a number of qualifying criteria, potentially including:

- **current qualification level.** The entitlement should only be available to those accessing a first, full Level 2 qualification;

- **qualifying period of work.** A minimum length of time an employee must have been in a job before they can access their entitlement; and

- **enforcement.** Whether there would be alternative ways for employers to satisfy regulation, such as allowing employees time off for training instead of participating in Train to Gain, before risking employment tribunals or other administrative mechanisms.

5.52 Introducing this new entitlement is likely to increase take-up of Train to Gain significantly. The international experience in Box 5.1 suggests that an increase in training by employers of up to 10 per cent provides a likely scenario, with increases dependent on the strength of the incentives for the employers to get involved. The Review expects take up of the entitlement to be at the top end of this spectrum given the flexible way in which training is delivered in Train to Gain. If, in the light of inadequate progress towards world class, the Commission and Government judge it as necessary, the new entitlement would ensure that the UK meets its 2020 ambition.

5.53 The proportion of the workforce eligible for the right will vary across regions, sectors and sizes of firm. For example, while nationally around 27 per cent of employees do not have at least a Level 2 qualification, in Wholesale and Retail the proportion is 37 per cent and in Financial Intermediation it is only 17 per cent. The total cost to an employer will vary accordingly, but as an illustration, an employer employing 18 people might expect to have four employees that are eligible for the entitlement, at a total cost of £1,100. The training takes on average 9 hours per month for 8 months. The public subsidy would cover the course and brokerage costs, as well as any wage compensation. On average this amounts to around £1,600 per learner.

5.54 By giving all employees the opportunity to acquire the functional literacy and numeracy skills they lack, and to achieve a Level 2 qualification through work, the UK will further release the potential of its workforce. Employees will have the skills, motivation, and support to respond to changing occupational skill demands and lengthening working lives. Employers will benefit from a workforce that is more flexible and better able to progress to higher skilled work, enabling and driving them to take advantage of the opportunities and challenges presented by globalisation. Shared action of this kind will deliver shared benefits.

WORLD-CLASS INTERMEDIATE AND HIGH SKILLS

5.55 Intermediate and high skills are increasingly critical to the success of business, with high private returns. The Review has recommended shifting the balance of intermediate skills to Level 3. This will partly be achieved by raising attainment at school. However, over 7 million people in work currently lack a Level 2 or above qualification and so the Review has proposed more than doubling attainment rates among adults, equating to an additional 1.9 million Level 3 attainments, including increasing the total number of Apprentices to 500,000.

5.56 Current action to improve the number of people with at least a Level 4 qualification is focused on increasing the number of young people going to university. The Review has recommended accelerating the drive to improve the proportion of adults with high skills, but broadening the focus so that there is more scope to increasing workplace skills among the adult population for businesses.

The current approach

5.57 There are clear and significant private returns to intermediate and high skills. The evidence in Chapter 1 showed that these levels of skill will increasingly drive productivity and prosperity in the global economy. Employers and individuals must be central in achieving the rates of improvement the Review has recommended.

Intermediate skills **5.58** One of the key current mechanisms for increasing employer investment in intermediate skills has been the expansion of Apprenticeships. Apprenticeships have traditionally been a major aspect of employer training in the UK – especially for young people – but the numbers of organisations offering them dropped steeply from the 1970s, associated with the decline in manufacturing employment.

5.59 Since that time the numbers of young people taking up Apprenticeships has grown dramatically from 75,000 in 1997 to 255,000 in 2005 in England alone. Currently around one quarter of 14-19 year olds undertake Apprenticeships of one form or another. However, the completion rate at 53 per cent is poor compared to 70 per cent through Train to Gain.[9] Government must take action to improve completion rates. The PSA target of having 175,000 young people starting an Apprenticeship during 2004-05 was exceeded, as was the Scottish

---

[9] *Further Education, work-based learning and adult and community learning - Learner numbers in England: 2005-06*, ONS, 2006

target of 30,000 on Modern Apprenticeships in 2004. There are targets for both participation and achievement – including increasing the numbers that achieve by at least 75 per cent between 2002/3 and 2007/8. The Government is currently ahead of trajectory towards achieving that target.

5.60   Employers are involved in the design of programmes and the 'hiring' of young people on Apprenticeships, but much of the content and programme is designed and funded by agencies such as the LSC, and other funding bodies in Scotland, Wales and Northern Ireland. As a result, employers now routinely claim that the Apprenticeship system is complex and bureaucratic and often does not meet their needs. This in turn contributes to the low achievement rates compared to other routes.

5.61   Apprenticeships are characterised by the apprentice being in employment, with much of the training delivered in the work place. Typically Apprenticeships are jobs with training, NVQs usually at Levels 2 or 3, technical certificates in the specialist work areas, and some wider skills such as Key Skills, often including literacy, numeracy and IT. In 2004, Apprenticeships were divided up into a series of levels; Young Apprenticeships for 14-16 year olds, Pre-Apprenticeships at Level 1, Apprenticeships at Level 2 and Advanced Apprenticeships at Level 3. At this time, the original age limit of 24 was removed and Adult Apprenticeships trialled.

5.62   Expanding the available levels and qualifying ages means that there are more Apprenticeships, but may dilute the overall brand. For many years Apprenticeships have been seen as the best possible route to obtaining practical vocational skills and a good job. This is borne out by the higher rates of return experienced by those taking up Apprenticeships, especially at Level 3. It is important that these levels of return and the esteem of Apprenticeships are maintained.

High skills   **5.63**   At the high skill level, Chapter 3 set out the Review's proposal to widen current efforts to improve high skills beyond their current sole focus on young people and to promote greater involvement by employers. Richard Lambert's 2003 Review of the links between higher education and business made the same arguments.[10] Its findings are summarised in Box 5.2.

---

[10] *Lambert Review of business-university collaboration*, HMSO, 2003.

Box 5.2: The Lambert Review

The Lambert Review analysed several aspects of the UK's HE system, but specifically concentrated on business-university collaboration. It considered the employability of UK graduates as well as the different drivers that influence the relationship between business and HE. Specifically, the Lambert Review found that:

- there is a mismatch between the needs of industry and the courses put on by universities in a particular area; and
- businesses find it difficult to engage with universities to enter a strategic dialogue about skills requirements.

This built on widespread employer concerns about the job readiness of graduates in the UK.

The Lambert Review recommended that Sector Skills Councils and RDAs work to address this:

- the Government should ensure that Sector Skills Councils have real influence over university courses and curricula. Otherwise, they will fail to have an impact on addressing employers' needs for undergraduates and postgraduates; and
- by refocusing HE courses and institutions.

The Review recommended that there was scope for other options and a need to increase the ability of SSCs and RDAs to influence the direction of HE.

5.64   Chapter 3 showed that the focus of higher education institutions now needs to be widened to encompass the whole working age population, given there is a clear risk that the existing funding prioritisation and the measurement of qualifying individuals towards the 50 per cent target still constrains this engagement. Furthermore, employers need clearer incentives and mechanisms to engage with and invest in HE. Without addressing these issues, the UK faces the risk that the productivity benefits from increasing the numbers of highly skilled adults are not fully realised. The highest levels of skills drive and facilitate innovation, leadership and management.

Going further

5.65   As the analysis above showed, Train to Gain is a successful method of delivering skills flexibly for employers in England. As recommended in Chapter 4, adult vocational skills funding in England should be delivered through Train to Gain and Learner Accounts by 2010. This will improve the quality of training employers can access and make it more flexible, leading to increased investment.

Apprenticeship support   **5.66**   Apprenticeships must meet the demands of employers. SSCs are currently involved in designing the frameworks and have input into qualification content. However, the LSC and QCA still have considerable control over content and funding. The role of employers, through SSCs, should be strengthened. As with qualifications, SSCs should control the content of Apprenticeships and set attainment targets by sector facilitated by skills brokers. This will enable them to simplify the Apprenticeship process and ensure that Apprenticeships meet employers' needs. As with qualifications it will ensure that Apprenticeships continue to be economically valuable, both to employers and individuals.

5.67   Employers, through SSCs, should be responsible for stimulating demand for Apprenticeships, and funding should be demand-led within the Train to Gain framework. This, along with advice from skills brokers, should help to increase the number of Apprenticeships to 500,000 a year across the UK. Employers should be encouraged to operate more 'bespoke' Apprenticeship programmes, innovatively delivered and with different types of funding incentives. SSCs should work closely with the appropriate funding bodies to see how overall apprenticeship funding can help support this approach.

5.68 The Government and Devolved Administrations should work with the Commission and SSCs to boost the number of people in the UK participating in Apprenticeships to 500,000 by 2020. The Government should build on the success of the Apprenticeship route, expanding it to become a pathway which is open to every suitably qualified 16-19 year old. It will always be a voluntary matter for employers to choose whether to offer apprenticeship places. Sector Skills Councils and skills brokers should work with employers to achieve the necessary increase in the supply of high quality places for young people and adults. As a result of this shared action, the Government should consider creating a new entitlement, as resources allow, so that every young person with the right qualifications should be able to take up an Apprenticeship place.

The role of SSCs **5.69** **The Review recommends that employers drive up attainment of intermediate and high skills, including in Apprenticeships, led by SSCs and skills brokers.** Through SSCs and skills brokers, employers will be better informed about where to get training, and what training they will find most valuable to meet their needs. They will also be better informed about longer-term challenges for their sectors, and the skills needed to meet those challenges. Where employers recognise these skills needs they should be responsible, through SSCs, for addressing these needs.

5.70 Chapter 4 set out the role for SSCs in considering collective measures to address sector specific skill needs. The mechanisms for addressing skill needs will vary by sector and even within sectors. The Review looks to key employers in each sector to be innovative in the approaches taken to address skill needs through SSCs. There are already many innovative schemes currently being developed by SSCs to address skill problems in their sectors, which range from projects with school children, to use of on-site training facilities to reach contract workers on large scale construction projects, to designing and subsidising degree courses. Partnerships with relevant trades unions, especially through the rapidly expanding Union Learning Representative network, will also be important and, through their board membership, SSCs will be able to utilise and build on this approach.

5.71 As articulated in Chapter 4, SSCs and skills brokers should be responsible for levering up employer engagement and investment in skills. **Sector Skills Agreements should include clear commitments and targets, including for the number of Apprenticeships, for increased employer achievement of intermediate and higher skills.** The Commission should scrutinise SSAs to ensure they are meeting the scale of this challenge.

5.72 As part of this, as at present, SSCs remain empowered to implement self-regulatory mechanisms to raise demand for skills across a sector where a clear majority of the employers in that sector support it. Levies already operate in the construction and film industries, as do licences to practise in many of the professions and other industries. **These measures should not be imposed by the Government.**

Demand led **5.73** Chapter 3 set out recommendations to change the targets faced by HE institutions **Higher Education** **to increase the focus on workforce development, away from a sole focus on participation in HE by young people.** This change will radically alter the incentives facing HE institutions, encouraging them to work with businesses in a way that they have not done to date. It is this change to incentives, rather than specific initiatives, which will drive the change in behaviour the Review has concluded is needed.

5.74 To further embed these incentives, the Review recommends that a portion of higher education funding in England be delivered through a similar demand-led mechanism as Train to Gain, as set out in Chapter 4. This should use Government funding to lever in greater investment by employers at Level 4 and above. This will change the incentives of HE providers to respond effectively to employer and individual demand. The Commission should monitor the relationship between HE and employers to make sure that the reforms recommended by the Review lead to a step change in collaboration. If they do not, the Commission should recommend new actions to be taken by employers and HE institutions.

5.75 While employer action to raise demand for intermediate and high skills should be driven by SSCs and the Commission, the Review has developed a specific proposal to increase employer engagement with universities. Improving the quality and quantity of senior research staff in higher education through employer collaboration and investment will facilitate greater levels of knowledge transfer, innovation and dialogue between leading employers and leading academic specialists in universities. These objectives must become important components of any assessment of research quality, as the system is developed to take the place of the Research Assessment Exercise (RAE).

Research Chairs programme **5.76** To further facilitate this, the Government should consider a programme of UK Research Chairs at junior and senior levels, building on and formalising the occasional links between employers and higher education and also the existing Wolfson and the proposed Royal Society Fellowship schemes. This replicates similar approaches in the US, Canada and Germany where university professors and senior researchers have their salaries topped up by a combination of employer and government funding.

CONCLUSION

5.77 This chapter has set out the recommended action between the Government and employers if the UK is to achieve its ambitions for 2020. At all levels, in return for employer influence over the content of qualifications and a change in the way skills are funded and delivered, employers will be expected to support and invest to address long term ambitions for the UK.

5.78 Without employer participation it will not be possible for the UK to achieve the scale of increase in skills levels that being world-class will require, as 70 percent of the 2020 workforce have already left school. Without a partnership between the Government and employers, businesses will lack the skilled workforce to adapt to technological change and succeed in the new global economy.

5.79 At lower levels of skill, the Review recommends additional voluntary action by employers to raise demand in line with the world class ambition. The Government and the Commission should judge in 2010 if the UK is on course for this ambition. If it is not, the Government should introduce a legal entitlement for low skilled workers to get training in the workplace, delivered through Train to Gain. At intermediate and high levels, employers must make hard commitments to increase investment, incentivised by public funding.

5.80 Increased engagement by employers is only part of the answer. The step change in skill levels will only be achieved with recognition from individuals that they are ultimately responsible for their training and progression. The Review's recommendations for achievement of greater individual engagement are set out in Chapter 6.

6 EMBEDDING A CULTURE OF LEARNING

Chapter summary

Previous chapters have set out the Review's proposals for a shared national mission for skills, recommendations to ensure that the skills and qualifications systems effectively deliver the needs of employers and individuals and a new partnership with employers based on a 'something for something' approach.

Individuals must be part of this shared national mission if the UK is to achieve world class skills, working with employers to improve their skills in work as well as investing in their own skills development outside work. This will require a step change in skills improvements by adults. The Review has found that a number of barriers constrain skills developments by individuals. Low aspirations and a low awareness of the benefits of skills mean that many people choose not to improve their skills even where it would benefit them. Lack of effective information and advice means that those who choose to learn do not have the help they need to make informed choices. Unclear financial support means that some people cannot afford to improve their skills. The quality of much provision varies considerably.

The Review proposes a new offer to individuals to further embed a culture of learning across society:

- raising aspiration. A new and sustained national campaign to raise career aspirations and awareness, backed by action in communities, increasing the appetite and opportunity to improve skills;

- making informed choices. In England, a new adult careers service, learning from those elsewhere in the UK, providing a universal source of labour-market focused and accessible careers advice for adults, including a free Skills Health Check;

- increasing choice. Giving individuals choice and control by entitling them to a Learner Account, learning from the schemes in Wales and Scotland, that they can use to pay toward the accredited learning of their choice; and

- ensuring people can afford to learn. Financial support based on the principles of clarity and targeting help to those who need it most. In England, a new Skills Development Fund, subsuming the Learner Support Fund, will tackle the immediate barriers for those wanting to improve their basic and Level 2 skills.

6.1   Developing a responsive, flexible skills system that delivers the skills employers need is an essential pre-requisite for meeting a world class ambition for skills. Individuals have to be part of a new, shared national mission, engaging in learning and investing where it will improve their pay and job prospects. This chapter sets out the Review's recommendations for tackling the barriers to learning and embedding an increased culture of learning across society.

THE CURRENT SITUATION: FALLING SHORT

6.2   Chapter 3 set out the scale of change necessary for the UK to achieve a world class skills base, more than doubling projected rates of improvement. The ambition is challenging and will require a step change in skills aspirations. The Review recommends a shared national mission for skills, recognising that both employers and individuals must have the incentives and the capability to improve their skills.

Raising attainment at school

6.3   This step change in aspirations must begin at school. Chapter 2 showed that, despite increases in recent years, a relatively low proportion of young people in the UK stay on in education or training past the age of 16. For example, in 2004, only 83 per cent of 17 year olds were enrolled in education or training, compared with 86 per cent in the USA and 97 per cent in Sweden.[1] Only 45 per cent of 15 year olds in schools achieve five or more grades A*-C including English and mathematics at GCSE or equivalent.[2]

6.4   Attainment in schools is unequally distributed. The UK has a relatively wide distribution of outcomes among the countries in the Organisation for Economic Co-operation and Development (OECD), with children from the poorest backgrounds far less likely to achieve good results compared with children from more advantaged backgrounds.[3] Only 13 per cent of young people entering full-time first degree courses at English higher education institutions in 2004-05 came from low participation neighbourhoods.[4] This unequal distribution of outcomes drives participation in learning by adults – those that have not achieved good results at school are far less likely to improve their skills as adults.

6.5   In turn, the strong links in the UK between the educational attainment of parents and their children means that the children of those who have not attained highly at school are also less likely to do well.[5] This creates a cycle of disadvantage that locks generations of the same family into persistent poverty. This cycle needs to be broken by both raising aspirations and standards in all schools, and ensuring that adults have a real and effective second chance to improve their skills.

Inequalities in skills

6.6   These inequalities in attainment have driven an unequal distribution of skills across the UK, shown in Chart 6.1. More than 33 per cent of people in the North East, Yorkshire and Humberside and the East Midlands have less than a Level 2 qualification, compared with around 28 per cent in the South East and Scotland. In Scotland and London more than 30 per cent of people hold at least a Level 4 qualification, compared to less than 25 per cent in Wales, Northern Ireland and the North East. Skills are also unequally distributed between groups of people. Over 40 per cent of those of working age with disabilities have no or low qualifications. More than 40 per cent of working age people of Asian or Asian British ethnicity hold only low or no qualifications, compared with 31 per cent of the white population.

---

[1] *Education at a glance 2006*, OECD, 2006.

[2] *Statistics for education: Education and training statistics for the United Kingdom*, DfES, 2005.

[3] *Programme for international student assessment*, OECD, 2000.

[4] *Performance indicators in higher education*, HESA, 2006.

[5] *Education and skills: The economic benefit*, DfES, 2003.

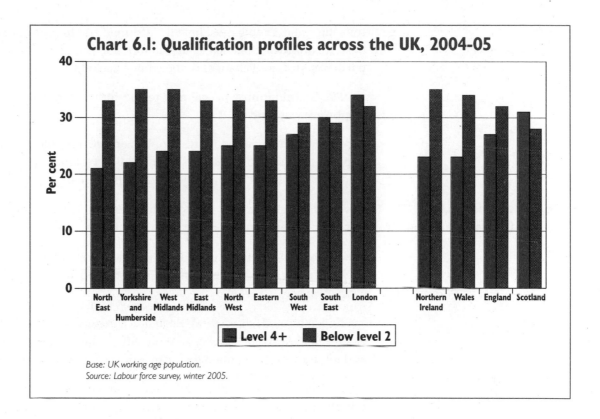

Chart 6.1: Qualification profiles across the UK, 2004-05

Base: UK working age population.
Source: Labour force survey, winter 2005.

6.7 The Review has found that patterns of adult skills development reinforce the current unequal distribution of skills:

- less than one half of adults (46 per cent) with no qualifications participate in any form of learning, compared with 92 per cent of those with a Level 4;

- 59 per cent of those with basic skills problems take part in learning compared with 85 per cent of those without;

- participation by those from low-income households is 26 percentage points lower than participation by those from high-income households (64 per cent relative to 90 per cent); and

- 31 per cent of those who were not learning in 2001 were doing some learning in 2003, compared to 84 per cent of those who were learning in 2001.[6]

Embedding a **6.8** Global economic changes, discussed in Chapter 1, are dramatically increasing the
culture of importance of skills. Ensuring a platform of skills and investing to update these skills as the
learning economy changes will increasingly determine people's pay and job prospects. Embedding a culture of learning across all groups in society will be essential to ensure that a world class skills base benefits everyone. This must begin at schools by delivering educational opportunity for all.

6.9 The Review has identified five key factors that underpin a culture of learning:

- aspiration and motivation. All individuals must be aware of the benefits from improving their skills and be both encouraged and motivated to do so;

---

[6] *National Adult Learning Survey 2005*, DfES, forthcoming and *Pathways in adult learning survey (PALS)*, DfES, 2003, which follows respondents to NALS 2001.

- fully informed. People must be fully informed and impartially advised of how best to improve their skills, based on the economic value attached to particular skills and changes in the labour market;

- choice. Learning must be tailored to the individual, delivered in a flexible responsive way; and

- appropriate financial support. People need to be able to afford to learn. Support to meet the costs of learning at all levels must be targeted at those who face the biggest barriers and credit constraints.

A new offer for   **6.10**   The Review recommends a new offer to adults to help further embed a culture of
individuals   learning across the country, ensuring everyone gets the help they need to get on in life:

- raising awareness and aspiration. A new and sustained national campaign, backed by action in communities, designed to lift aspirations and build awareness across society;

- making informed choices. In England, a new national careers service to ensure that everyone has access to the advice they need to improve their pay and job prospects and build their career in a changing labour market;

- increasing choice. Giving individuals real purchasing power by channelling all funding for individuals through Learner Accounts, which they can use to put toward the accredited learning of their choice; and

- ensuring individuals can afford to learn. Financial support based on the principles of clarity and targeting help to those who need it most. In England, a new Skills Development Fund will tackle the immediate barriers for those wanting to improve their basic and Level 2 skills.

6.11   The principles underlying this offer are not restricted to adults. A culture of learning must encompass all age groups if it is to be sustained beyond 2020. Effective careers advice in schools and colleges, combined with appropriate financial support, is needed to ensure young people are able to fully develop their talents.

RAISING ASPIRATION AND AWARENESS

6.12   For people to consider improving their skills, they need to be aware of and motivated by the benefits of doing so. They must see a link between skills development and achieving their own personal ambitions, such as improving their career, or being able to help their children with their homework. On its own, an abstract knowledge that learning can deliver higher wages will not be effective. For awareness to translate into action, people must be able to make informed choices so that they invest wisely. They need access to good quality, impartial information and advice on local learning opportunities and their relevance in the labour market.

6.13   Raising aspirations and awareness is a key challenge. Surveys point to a number of attitudinal barriers including a lack of interest in learning and a lack of confidence about going back to the classroom. Practical barriers, such as lack of time (particularly for those in work), are also important. Effective information and advice can help to explain the flexible learning opportunities on offer. 26 per cent of non-learners gave a lack of knowledge of local learning opportunities as a reason for not learning.[7]

---

[7] *National Adult Learning Survey*, DfES, 2002.

6.14 This applies to young people as well as adults. Recent research found that when students have access to effective careers guidance they tend to make more structured and informed decisions regarding their education.[8] It concluded that too few young people at age 14 are making the link between careers guidance and their personal decisions.

Current help **6.15** This lack of information is a clear market failure and there have been a number of attempts to raise aspirations and awareness of the importance of skills development, both among adults and at school. Several national campaigns have combined media advertising with local action to motivate and challenge adults, examples of which are summarised in Box 6.1. Similar schemes have targeted young people. Skills competitions can promote excellence in vocational skills. The World Skills 2011 competition will be held in London and is an opportunity to raise public understanding of the importance of skills and celebrate outstanding achievement.

Box 6.1: National learning campaigns

There have been a number of national campaigns aimed at raising awareness of the benefits of learning and the opportunities to learn. One of the best known is DfES' Gremlins campaign, launched in 2001, which challenged people on their basic skills needs. Almost 300,000 contacted the learndirect advice line after the campaign, 26 per cent of whom took up learning opportunities.

Following this success, learndirect launched a further campaign aimed at increasing learning in its network of learning centres in 2004. Afterwards, it saw a substantial increase in take-up resulting in 365,000 courses being taken, over 100,000 more than a year earlier.

The BBC has played a key role in educational campaigns. The latest campaign, in partnership with learndirect, is RAW (Reading and Writing), which hopes to *'inspire the 12 million adults in this country who struggle with everyday reading and writing skills'*. The first phase of the campaign sought to raise awareness through local RAW centres, complemented by national initiatives such as World Book Day and programmes like Test the Nation. Support is provided through a website, telephone helpline and mobile phone service. The campaign is now in its second stage, helping adults get into reading.

There are also several other campaigns focused on increasing learning among specific groups. These include the Education Maintenance Allowance campaign targeted at young people, the Apprenticeships campaign, which aims to improve awareness among employers as well as individuals, and a campaign raising awareness of Foundation Degrees.

6.16 Following an awakening of aspirations, people must be able to make informed choices. In England, information and advice on learning and careers is currently provided through a number of channels:

- learndirect. Provides information and advice on learning and careers through a phone line and website. The learndirect brand is well established, with 82 per cent brand recognition. Recently it launched a new telephone guidance service on a trial basis with the capacity to deliver 70,000 guidance sessions per year;

- nextstep. Provides face-to-face advice and information on learning and skills at a series of centres in each of the 47 local Learning and Skills Council (LSC) areas;

---

[8] *How do young people make choices at 14 and 16?*, Blenkinsop et al, 2006.

- Jobcentre Plus. Gives advice and help on finding work, including skills where appropriate, to those on benefits;

- Union Learning Representatives. More than 15,000 ULRs and 450 Union Learning Fund projects have helped over 67,000 learners access courses every year;[9]

- colleges and universities. Most colleges and universities provide a range of information and guidance services; and

- private and voluntary providers. Over 1,600 public, private, voluntary and community sector organisations have achieved the national quality standard for information, advice and guidance services (IAG).

6.17   Such services have helped to increase learning participation. The LSC found that 76 per cent of those who moved into learning following advice believe that service to be crucial or important in making the decision and transition.[10]

6.18   Some of these services, such as nextstep, do not operate on a UK-wide basis. Box 6.2 summarises services in the Devolved Administrations (DAs). The system for young people also differs across the UK. In England, Connexions is the Government's support service for young people aged 13 to 19. Through multi-agency working, Connexions provides information, advice, guidance and access to personal development opportunities for young people. It aims to remove barriers to learning and progression and ensure young people make a smooth transition to adulthood and working life. In the DAs, there is one service for those of all ages.

Box 6.2: Careers Advice in the Devolved Administrations

Northern Ireland, Scotland and Wales each have a nationally branded careers services, aimed at people of all ages.

Careers Scotland provides an all-age service for people at any stage in their career. It helps individuals to 'look at the changing labour market and career options, consider opportunities to learn and to get a job, and find sources of support'.[a] Advisors based in Careers Scotland centres assist individuals with their interview skills or help brush up their CV as well as providing detailed information and advice on job profiles and exploring education and training options. Careers Scotland also provides advice to employers and the learning and community sector.

Like Careers Scotland, Careers Wales is an all-age careers service. It also works with a variety of organisations including employers and other organisations in the sector. Their website offers online guidance tools, job vacancy search facilities and the Learning Choices database, which provides information on over 43,000 courses and training opportunities throughout Wales. Alternatively, the individual can meet a careers advisor, located in colleges and local careers centres.

Careers Service Northern Ireland base their careers advisors in their Jobcentres and Jobs and Benefit Offices, as well as in Careers Centres. Complementing this face-to-face service is a website providing information on careers and improving skills, which also has a link to the Jobcentre Plus job search database, allowing users to see what local job vacancies exist.

[a] www.careers-scotland.org.uk.

---

[9] *Changing lives through learning, a guide to unionlearn*, unionlearn, 2006.
[10] *The impact of adult information and advice services – a summary*, LSC, 2003.

Problems with the current system

6.19 The current system in England is fragmented and fails to integrate advice on learning with careers advice. In a recent evaluation, over one third of people who sought skills advice or guidance wanted to find out about career opportunities.[11] The current system, particularly in England, provides advice on different aspects of building a career in silos, with Jobcentre Plus providing help in getting a job and providers of skills advice able to help with finding a particular course. Nowhere is this brought together so that people are advised how to effectively build their job and pay prospects. Skills development is not set in the context of people's aspirations.

6.20 Even advice focused purely on skills is fragmented. In England, learndirect and nextstep provide similar services aimed at similar groups, but under different brands and organisations. The Adult Learning Inspectorate (ALI) review of learndirect advice in 2005 identified this as a principal area for development and improvement.[12] They noted that competition between learndirect advice and nextstep is hindering the development of an integrated Information Advice and Guidance (IAG) service for adults.

6.21 As recognised in the Government's Skills White Paper of March 2005, this fragmentation is one of the sources of complexity for people and leaves them unclear where to go for help.[13] Consequently, widespread lack of awareness of the benefits of and options for learning remain. As the global economy changes and skills requirements change and rise, people will increasingly need to access effective advice on how to stay in work and progress.

The Review's proposals: raising aspirations

6.22 The Review has developed fresh recommendations to raise awareness and aspiration among adults across society. At the heart of these is a new universal careers service for England to give people the advice they need to progress in the modern labour market and adapt to change. This will bring together current separate sources of advice and draw them out of their silos. The Review recommends that this service operate under the already successful and well-known learndirect brand. **It will retain the current learndirect budget and also subsume the nextstep budget. It must draw on Jobcentre Plus information and services, so that information on jobs, skills and training can be integrated.** This service will be directly responsible for raising participation in learning and so should be accountable to and managed by the DfES.

6.23 The new service will be responsible for:

- integrated delivery. Advice delivered through a number of channels and locations, including co-location with Jobcentres to provide a high profile place to go for job search facilities and employment and skills advice;

- integrated advice. Careers advice based on local labour market information;

- effective screening. Everyone entitled to a free Skills Health Check to assess their skills needs;

- proactive. Reaching out rather than waiting for people to come. The service will be rewarded for raising participation rather than through a block grant; and

---

[11] *Intermediate impacts of advice and guidance*, DfES, 2006.

[12] *Inspection Report, learndirect advice*, ALI, 2005.

[13] *Skills: Getting on in business, getting on at work*, DfES, 2005.

- accessibility. Advice delivered through multiple channels, including the internet and a phone line, at a time and location suited to the individual.

Raising aspirations   **6.24**   The new adult careers service will be charged with raising aspiration and awareness of the importance and benefits of learning, particularly among those that have missed out in the past. It will lead a sustained national campaign to promote skills development among groups that would not normally consider learning.

6.25   This national campaign must be backed up by local action in communities. The Review recognises that the success of national publicity campaigns, such as the DfES Gremlins campaign summarised in Box 6.1, has depended on local activity. Many skills and careers advisors have forged strong links with local community organisations, allowing them to promote skills and careers development further and to deliver advice flexibly in community centres, as well as dedicated advice centres. The careers service will build on the many existing partnerships with local organisations, engaging the hardest to reach.

6.26   Experience has shown the importance of integrating campaigns with an effective information and advice service. Knowledge of the benefits of learning is not enough. There is a clear demand from people for advice on how they can use learning to improve their career, which the new careers service will supply. Having an expert knowledge of the local labour market and being able to draw on information and services from Jobcentre Plus, will enable advisors to inform individuals of the local career opportunities and the skills employers are looking for.

6.27   Effective careers guidance is particularly important for young people, so that they can make the best start to their working life. Services like Connexions and careers advisors in schools are essential to raising career and learning ambitions and ensuring young people can make informed decisions.

Skills Health Check   **6.28**   Unless people are aware of their own skills needs, they will not be able to tackle them. At the heart of the new service will be the offer of a full assessment of people's skills in the context of the career they wish to develop. The Review recommends that all adults should be entitled to a free 'Skills Health Check', building on the success of a similar approach in Sweden, that would identify an individual's skill needs and strengths. People should be able to access this by contacting the new careers service. Following on from this, advisers will ensure that people are advised on the most effective action, whether that is going on a course, doing work experience or learning at work, to tackle their needs and develop their career.

Flexible delivery   **6.29**   Careers advice should be delivered at a time suitable for the individual, not just tied to the working day. Advisors will be conveniently co-located with employment services in town and city centres, as well as in the community, colleges and other locations. Rather than paid solely though a block grant, local advice centres will be rewarded for raising participation, encouraging them to deliver a service that engages the hard-to-reach.

6.30   A range of other sources of information and advice will remain important. For example, services in colleges, private providers and the network of 15,000 Union Learning Representatives all make an immensely valuable contribution. The careers services in the Devolved Administrations are already based on many of these principles. In developing their careers services further, the Devolved Administrations should look to further embed the approach set out above.

IMPROVING CHOICE

6.31   Chapter 3 outlines the importance of a learning environment that is driven by individuals' and employers' demands. It recommends that all adult skills vocational funding in England, excepting that for adult community learning and services for those with learning difficulties and disabilities, be channelled through Train to Gain and Learner Accounts in England by 2010. Train to Gain gives employers control over their learning. Employers can choose a learning provider of their choice and receive subsidised training that is tailored to their skill needs. Employees in turn benefit from training delivered at the workplace, in skills that their employer values.

6.32   People choosing to learn outside the workplace, whether for personal benefit or to build a new career, should have the same degree of control. At present, the LSC, rather than the learner, decides the amount of funding a college receives and the type of learning it should deliver. The result is a learning environment that often responds to the LSC's demands instead of the learner's.

Learner Accounts **6.33**   Learner Accounts provide people with virtual funding to use at an accredited learning provider of their choice. By channelling funding through the learner, individuals have real purchasing power over their learning. From Autumn 2007, DfES will be running pilots of Learner Accounts for individuals studying for a Level 3 qualification. Both Scotland and Wales operate similar schemes, targeted at lower levels of learning. These, along with the previous Individual Learning Account scheme in England, are discussed in Box 6.3.

Box 6.3: Learner Accounts

Learner Accounts, sometimes called Individual Learning Accounts (ILA), provide people with funding that they can spend at an accredited learning provider of their choice.

Individual Learning Accounts were introduced in England in 2000 with the aim of encouraging people back into learning, particularly young adults with few qualifications. Various financial incentives were used to attract learners and the scheme proved immensely popular with over 1.4 million accounts being used. The majority of learners already had a Level 2 qualification. Unfortunately, the ILA programme closed in 2001 after receiving allegations of serious potential fraud.

ILA Scotland was launched in December 2004, with an initial offer targeted at low-income learners, that provides up to £200 to fund a wide range of courses. Low income is defined as earnings below £15,000 per annum. The aims of the scheme are to introduce new people into adult learning and to encourage individuals to invest in and take ownership of their own learning. A further, universal offer of £100 was introduced in 2005, which provides up to £100 for learners on a basic skills or ICT course.

Wales has targeted its ILA at the low skilled and benefit recipients. Like Scotland, Wales encourages individual investment in learning and provides funding for half of course costs, up to £100. This is for non-benefit recipients with qualifications below Level 3. Benefit recipients are eligible for up to £200. The scheme has been particularly successful at attracting new adult learners. 35 per cent of account holders, for example, had not participated in learning within the last five years or since leaving school.

In Autumn 2007, DfES will start piloting Learner Accounts for learners studying at Level 3. Account holders will be entitled to a discount on the cost of a Level 3 course that reflects the national fee rate set by the LSC for that year, currently 62.5 per cent. Like any account, learners will receive an account statement that sets out the various contributions by the individual and the state, as well as any learner support the learner is receiving.

The Review's proposals: improving choice and quality

6.34 The recent Education and Skills Select Committee report on further education endorsed the reintroduction of Learner Accounts and noted that problems marring the previous Individual Learning Account scheme were administrative rather than fundamental.[14] The Review supports this conclusion, recognising that learning accounts present real benefits for people, increasing ownership and choice, as well as providing a powerful incentive to the supply-side to drive up quality.

6.35 The similar schemes in Scotland and Wales have successfully shown that accounts can be expanded to learners at lower learning levels and the Review wants to ensure that all learners, particularly those most likely to be disengaged from learning, can access the benefits that accounts deliver. The new careers service will play a key role in ensuring an informed and demanding customer group.

Learner Accounts **6.36** The majority of adult skills funding should be targeted on work-focused learning delivered through Train to Gain. However, people will continue to want to learn outside work too, whether to train for a new career or for personal reasons. The Review recommends that all adult vocational further education funding for individuals in England, including the current Level 2 entitlement, be channelled through Learner Accounts by 2010. In this way, all adult further education funding will be demand-led – through Train to Gain for employers and Learner Accounts for individuals. These accounts should not be based on providing colleges with a block grant based on expected demand and clawing back the difference at the end of the academic year. Instead, colleges should receive full funding only when individuals enrol on and complete a course. This will give the best providers freedom to expand, while encouraging all providers to be more responsive to the demands of their customers – in this case, individuals.

6.37 The Learner Account pilots have safeguards to reduce the risk of fraud. Learners, for instance, will only be able to attend accredited learning providers and funding in the accounts is virtual (i.e. actual funding will be channelled through the existing provider payments system, rather than held in the accounts). Within these constraints, learners are free to choose where they want to study. Effective providers can quickly expand since each new learner brings extra funding. Likewise, poor providers will be forced to raise their quality or face exiting the market. In this way, Learner Accounts will drive up quality and flexibility, as well as giving individuals greater choice and power.

6.38 Over time, the Government should consider rolling other forms of financial support into these accounts, such as the learner support discussed in the following section and any childcare support. Incentives could be given for finance from the Child Trust Fund to be used for learning. This would give individuals their own account, made up of real money, and with incentives for them to make their own contribution. They would then have very real choice about how to use this to manage their own skills development, in the same way that individual accounts are giving people choice over their social care.[15]

EFFECTIVE FINANCIAL SUPPORT

6.39 Raising aspirations and ensuring people are fully informed and able to make choices about their careers and options for improving skills, must be backed up by action to ensure they can afford to learn. Learning can involve significant costs and one fifth of non-learners

---

[14] *Further Education, Fourth Report of the Session 2005-06*, Education and Skills Select Committee, 2006.

[15] *Independence, well-being and choice: Our vision for the future of social care for adults in England*, Department of Health, 2005.

said a lack of funding was a reason for not learning.[16] Course fees, childcare and transport are just some of the potential costs that learners face. In addition, people may have to reduce their hours at work to attend training. These costs, without adequate support, can make learning prohibitive.

6.40   Many people, particularly those on low incomes, are unable or unwilling to finance these costs, in the expectation of improved pay and job prospects after they have completed a course. Just under one half of all households have less than £1,500 in savings and over one quarter have no savings at all.[17] Financial support or additional credit is necessary for people on the lowest incomes.

6.41   In addition, while the average return to education is high, people face uncertainty about the benefit they will gain. For example, wage returns to a Level 2 qualification vary from zero to 23 per cent, depending on type of course, gender and level of prior education.[18] Many new learners also start out apprehensive over the course difficulty, questioning whether they will be able to pass the course, especially if they did not achieve at school.

Current help **6.42**   In response, the Government has introduced a range of measures to alleviate the direct and indirect costs of improving skills, targeting support at those who face the highest barriers. To reduce the direct course fee costs, the Government has:

- made all basic skills courses free;

- introduced a Level 2 entitlement, so that those who do not have a full Level 2 qualification can gain one for free;

- introduced a Level 3 entitlement for those under the age of 25 who do not have a full Level 3 qualification;

- partially subsidised course fees for those over the age of 25 undertaking a Level 3 and all those taking a Level 4, as set out in Chapter 3, as well as part Level 2 and 3 courses and training where the individual is already qualified to a higher level; and

- in higher education, full-time undergraduates are eligible for a Student Loan for fees, which becomes repayable only after their course has finished and when their income exceeds £15,000 a year. Low income students now benefit from a grant for living costs of up to £2,700 a year, as well as bursaries from higher education institutions. Part-time students may be eligible for a means tested grant towards tuition fees and a grant of up to £250 towards course costs.

6.43   Support is also available to meet indirect costs of learning, such as transport, childcare and course expenses, such as books:

- full-time learners on low incomes who are not on out-of-work benefits, studying for a first full Level 2 or 3 qualification are entitled to the Adult Learning Grant (ALG), which will shortly be rolled out nationwide, worth up to £30 per week;

- those adult learners on vocational courses who are not eligible for fee remission can also take out a Career Development Loan (CDL), a deferred

---

[16] *National Adult Learning Survey*, DfES, 2002.

[17] *Family Resources Survey*, 2004-05.

[18] *An in-depth analysis of the returns to National Vocational Qualifications obtained at Level 2*, Dearden et al, CEE, 2004.

repayment bank loan used to pay for tuition fees, but which may also help with living costs; and

- for the most disadvantaged learners, the LSC distributes a Learner Support Fund (LSF) worth £120 million per year to colleges to give out on a discretionary basis, providing assistance for costs such as childcare, transport, books and equipment, and to meet any financial problems people face while they are learning.

6.44   This support is helping many people who would not otherwise be able to afford to study to do so. The LSF supports around 220,000 adults per year with the majority of recipients coming from areas with the highest level of disadvantage.[19] The ALG is forecast to support 30,000 adults per year when fully rolled out. In 2005-06 a public budget of £17 million for CDLs supported a total allocation by private banks of £85.9 million to over 17,800 new learners.

6.45   Young people also have access to financial support. The Education Maintenance Allowance (EMA) pays up to £30 a week to those who continue to stay on in education after 16. It aims to increase participation by individuals who would otherwise be attracted to going straight into work. Evaluation has found that, among eligible young people, the allowance increased the proportion who were in full-time education at ages 16 and 17 by 6.1 percentage points.[20] The programme had the largest positive impact upon young people from low-income families and young men, two groups that tend to be under-represented in post-16 education. Income-contingent loans and limited grants are available to help students with HE course and living costs.

Devolved **6.46**   The Devolved Administrations have introduced their own systems of financial
Administrations support. Scotland operates a system of means-tested, discretionary bursaries for students in further and higher education. Full-time further education students can receive up to £80.74 per week to cover living costs. Further allowances are available to cover additional costs including materials costs, childcare and travel. Further Education students in Wales can be eligible for Financial Contingency Funds, similar to the English Learner Support Funds, designed to meet the costs of books, travel, childcare, accommodation or general living expenses. Career Development Loans are available in both Wales and Scotland. Northern Ireland has a range of discretionary further education awards.

Problems with **6.47**   The Review recognises the valuable contribution made by the current system of
the current financial support. However, it has found that existing support could be more effectively used.
system Financial concerns and uncertainty over financial support are some of the biggest barriers for people, yet current support is often unclear and uncertain.

6.48   At present, most financial support, except in the case of higher education, is marketed by learning providers to existing learners. For example, colleges allocate the LSF on a discretionary basis to support those already in learning. The Review has concluded that the lack of transparency and uncertainty over the Learner Support Fund acts as a real disincentive for the hardest to reach. Since it is discretionary, potential learners cannot be sure whether they will receive help and how much they might get.

6.49   As a result, the evaluation of the LSF found that students have very limited, and often non-existent, knowledge or understanding of the funds before they go to college.[21] Even once

---

[19] *Learner Support Funds: Second evaluation final report*, Institute for Employment Studies, 2005.

[20] *Evaluation of Education Maintenance Allowance pilots: Young people aged 16 to 19 years, final report of the quantitative evaluation*, DfES Research Report 678, 2005.

[21] *Evaluation of Learner Support Funds*, Institute for Employment Studies, 2003.

enrolled on a course, colleges may not advertise the funds. For example, the LSF evaluation highlighted concerns among providers that they would stimulate demand that they could not meet. Other providers could not advertise the LSF in their prospectus because they did not know how much funding from the LSC they would receive.

6.50 In addition, financial support varies considerably according to level of study and age, rather than purely by need. For example, the system of EMAs for young people is similar to, but not the same as, the ALG for older learners, even where people may be on the same course and in the same financial position. The system for HE differs still further.

The Review's proposals: effective financial support

6.51 Financial support should be aimed at those who most need it. Those that can afford to pay for skills development should do so. Financial support must also be clear, giving people a firm expectation of the support they will receive before they enrol on a course.

6.52 The Review proposes a new system of financial support, based on the principle of transparency and building on best practice elsewhere:

- clear and transparent financial support for those considering skills development as well as for existing learners; and

- greater use of Career Development Loans particularly for those looking to progress to intermediate level and beyond.

Upfront support   **6.53** The Learner Support Fund supports existing learners, but people have little or no idea of the support they will receive until after enrolment. For people thinking about improving their skills, but uncertain about whether they can afford to do so, this uncertainty acts as an unnecessary barrier. The Review recommends that a Skills Development Fund (SDF) replace the LSF. Based on clear eligibility criteria developed by the new service, advisers should use this fund flexibly to tackle the immediate financial barriers to learning that potential and current learners face. The new careers service should actively promote the new transparent criteria. In this way, the SDF will tackle the financial barriers to learning. Individuals will have a clearer understanding of support before they enrol on a course, while those already in learning have access to support if they face unexpected financial pressures.

6.54 The SDF will resemble the Advisor Discretion Fund (ADF) operated by Jobcentre Plus. Under the ADF, Jobcentre Plus advisers can grant jobseekers up to £100 to tackle the immediate barriers to finding work, such as travel to interview and buying smart clothes. Similarly, the Skills Development Fund will be used by advisers in the new careers service to tackle the immediate costs to enrolling in learning, such as transport and books, with support considered on a case-by-case basis but backed by clear, publicised criteria.

Career   **6.55** People looking to progress to Level 3 will, on average, gain a larger private return than
Development   those studying at lower levels. They will also tend to have better job and pay prospects. It is
Loans   right that they bear a greater share of the costs than those below Level 2. Chapter 3 set out the Review's analysis that employers and individuals should bear at least one half of the costs of Level 3.

6.56 Career Development Loans allow people to pay for their learning by covering any short-term credit constraints. They lever in private investment and are flexible, allowing funding for any course that the individual and bank judge will gain returns. At present the low cap on initial public funds used to lever in private funding prevents the scheme from reaching its full potential. The Review recommends that the Government consider raising the cap on initial public funds so that more people, in particular at higher levels, can invest in their own skills development. Further measures, such as greater use of payment and interest holidays, should be introduced to ensure that people have more effective insurance against the risk of not improving their wage and job prospects.

6.57   The Review's recommendations are specific to England, but in many cases build on experience elsewhere in the UK. In the longer-term, the Government and the Devolved Administrations should look to embed the same set of principles across all financial support for learning. It should look to better integrate and rationalise existing systems of support into Learner Accounts, discussed above.

CONCLUSION

6.58   The ambitions set out in Chapter 3 require a step change in skills development by individuals. This chapter has set out evidence that there is much further to go to further embed a culture of learning across all groups in society. Raising aspirations and ambitions among traditionally disadvantaged groups, particularly those who have not succeeded at school, is a key challenge.

6.59   Following on from this, a highly fragmented information and advice system, largely removed from the local labour market context, means people find it difficult to be informed about the opportunities available and their economic value. Financial support for those unable to pay the costs of learning is bedevilled by uncertainty and lack of clarity, and people's choice and control is heavily constrained by a funding system that does not reflect learner's demands.

6.60   The Review recommends a new offer to people to embed a culture of learning across society. At the heart of this is a national campaign, backed by local action, to raise aspiration and awareness. This will be driven by a new national adult careers service in England, drawing current sources of support into one place and offering everyone a Skills Health Check to assess their skills needs. It will be backed by action to ensure clear and targeted financial support and giving people choice and control by entitling them to a Learner Account.

6.61   The next chapter sets out how skills advice and services can be better integrated with employment advice and services. In this way, the drive to a world class skills base can contribute to the drive to world class employment and an 80 per cent employment rate.

7 EMPLOYMENT AND SKILLS

Chapter summary

In Budget 2006, the Chancellor commissioned the Leitch Review to consider how to better integrate skills and employment services. In the new global economy, people's economic security can no longer come from trying to protect particular jobs, holding back the tide of change. Instead, it comes from helping people adapt to change, finding new work and opportunities. Skills are increasingly central to world class employment and building the flexibility that delivers economic security.

The Review has found that significant reforms are needed to ensure employment and skills services effectively help people meet this new challenge. Current skills and employment services have different aims which means that delivery can be complex with an array of agencies trying to give help and advice to people. As a result, people do not receive the full support they need and are unsure how and where to access it. The risk is people will be trapped in worklessness or low paid jobs, lacking the support they need to get into and stay in work and progress.

To ensure people can access an integrated employment and skills service, the Review recommends:

- a **new programme to help benefit claimants with basic skills problems. Including a new programme to screen all benefit claimants, and more help to improve their basic skills;**

- a **new universal adult careers service, providing labour market focused careers advice for all adults. The new careers service will deliver advice in a range of locations, including co-location with Jobcentre Plus, drawing on Jobcentre Plus information and services, creating a national network of one stop shops for careers and employment advice;**

- a **new integrated objective for employment and skills services of sustainable employment and progression. Meeting this will require all involved in such services, from Departments, the LSC and Jobcentre Plus, to front line staff and colleges, to focus on people's long-term, as well as short-term, prospects; and**

- a **network of employer-led Employment and Skills Boards to give employers a central role in recommending improvements to local services, mirroring the national role of the Commission for Employment and Skills. The Boards will work to ensure that local services meet employer needs and the workless are equipped to access work.**

As a result of these recommendations, everyone claiming benefits will have their basic skills assessed and be offered help if they need it. When they find work, they will be linked into in-work support. People who find it more difficult to find or stay in work will be offered more intensive support, including help with their skills. All adults, including those in work, will be able to access work-focused careers advice, giving them the support they need to get on in work. This will contribute to increases in sustainable employment and progression, as well as reductions in child poverty.

7.1   In Budget 2006, the Leitch Review was commissioned by the Chancellor of the Exchequer to *'consider a far reaching proposal under which Britain can lead in skills: whether and how to bring together at a local level employment and training services for not just the unemployed, but all seeking new skills'*. This chapter sets out how an integrated employment and skills service is essential to ensure people get the help they need to find work, stay in employment and get on in their career in the modern labour market. In this way, the UK can achieve both world class skills and world class employment, rather than being forced to falsely choose between the two.

THE SCALE OF THE CHALLENGE

Worklessness and skills **7.2** The UK's employment rate, at almost 75 per cent, is one of the highest in the G7. However, there are still large numbers of people who find it difficult to find work and many of these have low or no skills. Around 1.7 million people are unemployed on the International Labour Organisation (ILO) definition. Almost one half (750,000) have less than a Level 2 qualification, of whom around 300,000 have no qualifications at all. Among the 7.8 million economically inactive in the UK working age population, almost one third, 2.2 million people, have no qualifications at all and almost one half, 3.7 million people, lack at least a Level 2. Around one quarter of disabled people have no qualifications.

7.3 Around 50 per cent of those with no qualifications are out of work. As the global economy changes, the employment opportunities of those lacking a platform of skills will fall still further. The millions of adults lacking functional literacy and numeracy skills risk becoming a lost generation, increasingly cut off from labour market opportunity. Equipping disadvantaged groups with a platform of skills, including literacy and numeracy, will be increasingly essential to improving their employment opportunities. The Government has identified work as the best route out of poverty, so tackling these problems can contribute to reductions in child poverty.

Sustainability of work **7.4** Most unemployed people move back into work quickly – nearly 80 per cent end their benefit claim within 6 months – and some degree of cycling will be inevitable in a flexible and dynamic labour market.[1] However, of the 2.4 million new Jobseeker's Allowance claims each year, around two thirds, or 1.6 million, are repeat claims. Those with low or no skills make up around one half of these, 800,000 claims. This means that one third of all JSA claims each year are repeat claims from those with low or no qualifications.

7.5 As the economy restructures in response to global economic changes, problems with employment retention are likely to worsen, particularly for the low skilled. Those falling out of work will find it increasingly difficult to move back into work unless they are able to update their skills in order to open up opportunities in the growing sectors of the economy. Unless people are able to update and improve their skills, they risk losing touch with the labour market, unable to find new jobs.

Progression **7.6** Many people moving into work become trapped in low paid, entry-level work. As Chapter 1 showed, social mobility is low in the UK and has fallen in recent decades. Those in low paid work tend to be those with low or no qualifications. Over one quarter of all employees, almost 7 million people, have less than a Level 2 qualification. Almost 2 million employees have no qualifications at all. Ensuring everyone has the opportunity to improve their skills is the best way to improve social mobility in the UK.

7.7 In the new global economy, economic security cannot be provided by trying to protect particular jobs, attempting to hold back the tide of change. Instead, economic security can only come from ensuring people have the support they need to stay in employment, taking new opportunities as they arise. Skills are a central part of this, equipping people with the flexibility they need to change jobs and careers as the economy changes. Increasingly, world class skills are essential to delivering world class employment and reduced child poverty. These are UK-wide challenges.

---

[1] *Budget 2006, A strong and strengthening economy: Investing in Britain's future*, HM Treasury, 2006.

THE CURRENT SYSTEM

7.8   There are a number of ways in which the Government seeks to help people improve their pay and job prospects. Chapter 4 set out the Review's recommendations to reform the delivery of skills to better meet the needs of individuals and employers. Jobcentre Plus is the key agency across Great Britain that seeks to help people find work.[2] It had an annual budget of around £1 billion in 2005-06 for Welfare to Work employment programmes, including the New Deals. Around one third of Welfare to Work provision is delivered through more than 1,000 contracts with the private and third sectors. While skills policy is devolved, employment policy is determined nationally.

Box 7.1: A brief overview of the Welfare to Work system

Jobcentre Plus, established in 2002 following the merger of the working age parts of the Benefits Agency and Employment Service, administers the benefit system. It aims to help people find work through the Jobseeker's Allowance (JSA) system for unemployed people and Work-Focused Interviews (WFIs) for those on other benefits, such as Incapacity Benefit and Income Support. It also provides a recruitment service to employers and for people seeking to change jobs.

More intensive support is provided through the New Deals. Young people aged 18 to 24 and claiming JSA for six months or more are enrolled in the New Deal for Young People (NDYP). This provides support, including training, to help people back into work. Evidence shows that without the NDYP, youth unemployment would have been twice as high.[a] Most claimants over the age of 24 are eligible for similar support through the ND25+ after 18 months claiming JSA.

The New Deal for Lone Parents (NDLP) has helped more than 420,000 lone parents into work, contributing one half of the 11 percentage point rise in the lone parent employment rate since 1997.[b] Recent pilots of extra support for disabled people, Pathways to Work, have successfully increased the rates that flow off benefit and are now being rolled out nationwide.[c] In most cases, Jobcentre Plus contracts New Deal provision from private and third sector providers. In 13 Employment Zones, employment support is delivered by private providers, rewarded for the outcomes they achieve.

---

[a] *The New Deal for young people: implications for employment and the public finances*, NIESR, 2000.

[b] *Welfare reform and lone parents employment in the UK*, CMPO working paper 72, Gregg and Harkness, 2003.

[c] For a discussion of the successful impact, see *Economic survey of the United Kingdom*, OECD, 2005.

Interlinked services **7.9**   There are a number of people for whom both skills and employment services need to work closely together. For example, people on benefits can access training where their Personal Adviser (PA) sees a lack of skills as a key barrier to finding work and the New Deals include a training option. At present there are estimated to be some 400,000 people on welfare benefits studying in FE.[3] A range of networks at national, regional and local levels attempt to ensure people get a joined-up service. These include Regional Skills Partnerships (RSPs), NEP employer coalitions, City Strategy pilots and Local Authority-led action through Local Strategic Partnerships. These initiatives are discussed more fully below. The institutional structure of delivery in England is illustrated in Chart 7.1. The linkages in the Devolved Administrations differ. In Scotland, an Employability Framework aims to ensure that Jobcentre Plus and skills services work effectively together.[4]

---

[2] Northern Ireland has a network of Jobs and Benefit Offices and Jobcentres.

[3] *Labour Force Survey*, ONS, Autumn 2005.

[4] *Workforce Plus – An employability framework for Scotland*, Scottish Executive, 2006.

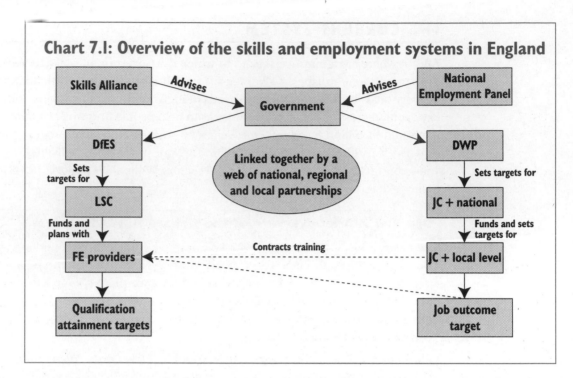

Chart 7.1: Overview of the skills and employment systems in England

7.10   The Review has found real strengths in the current employment and skills systems. The Welfare to Work system successfully helps people find work and the skills system is good at helping people attain qualifications. However, the evidence set out above shows that many people find it difficult to stay in work and progress, and that others, particularly in disadvantaged groups, find it difficult to find work. These problems are likely to become more pronounced as the global economy changes and contribute to child poverty.

7.11   The Review has found that disjoints between skills and employment services mean they cannot give people the full support they need to overcome these problems. The skills system is largely separate from the employment system and both work to different goals: entry into jobs for the employment system and full qualification attainment for the skills system. This means they do not work together as effectively as they could, with policies not complementary and delivery fragmented. As a result, people get a disjointed service: skills improvements are not effectively used to help people who need them to find work or progress, skills policy is not focused enough on improving employability and support is not joined up across the transition to work.

Local and regional complexity

Existing local and regional arrangements   7.12   The fragmented service that people receive is particularly apparent at the sub-national level, with a wide array of bodies trying to plan services in a way that will meet expected need. As discussed in Chapter 4, skills delivery is currently planned to meet expected demand by the LSC nationally, regionally and locally. The RDAs lead on Regional Skills Partnerships (RSPs), which aim to ensure that planning of skills meets regional economic needs.

7.13 To ensure these plans fit with local need and delivery of other services, a range of other planning bodies have been created. Local Learning and Skills Councils have employers represented at board level, though the recent FE Bill proposes replacing these with similar regional councils. The DWP have introduced a series of City Strategies across the UK aimed at increasing employment rates through partnership. These operate at a variety of geographic levels and tend to include a strong focus on skills.[5] Some include employers, others do not.

7.14 Local Authorities too, have an interest in skills and employment services and several, such as Manchester, Liverpool and Nottingham, have developed Skills Boards, operating alongside, or as a part of, their Local Strategic Partnership (LSP) arrangements. LSPs are intended to allow providers of a range of services, from health to skills, to come together and ensure they work effectively together. In London, a Skills and Employment Board, chaired by the Mayor of London, is developing a strategy for adult training that will drive the allocation of LSC vocational training funds for London. It is expected that the Board will largely replace the London RSP.

7.15 Alongside this, for employment policy the NEP oversees a network of Employer Coalitions across the UK advising on local needs. These coalitions were established in 1998 in ten areas; Birmingham, Derbyshire, Glasgow, Greater Manchester, Highland, London, Merseyside, North East England, South Yorkshire and West Yorkshire. NEP also operates a series of Fair Cities programmes designed to improve the employment rates of ethnic minorities in Birmingham, Bradford and Brent.[6]

Impact **7.16** This proliferation of initiatives confuses employers and leaves them unclear as to where they should engage at a local level in order to influence the delivery of skills and employment services, in the same way as Chapter 2 showed they are unclear at the national and sectoral level. It means that services are denied the effective input of employers and consequently people do not receive a service that would maximise their employability and progression.

7.17 Too many current bodies are focused on planning and inputting into central design. As Chapter 2 showed, planning has a historically weak record of meeting economic needs. Too often, collective articulation of future skills needs has been an ineffective and inefficient mechanism. Consequently, people do not get the full range of effective labour market support they need. The approaches that work to improve skill services are invariably demand-led, with providers of services only rewarded when they meet the needs of individual employers and people, rather than trying to plan to pre-empt these needs.

The need for better integration **7.18** Skills are not always the magic bullet for improving employment and career progression. Most workless people face a range of barriers to finding work. For example, the employment rate for those with no qualifications and no disability is around 59 per cent, but falls to around 21 per cent for those who are both disabled and unqualified.[7] Similarly, improved employment is not the only potential outcome from improving skills. People are also motivated by personal achievement, alongside a range of other factors.

---

[5] City Strategies currently in place include Birmingham, Blackburn, Dundee, East London, Edinburgh, Glasgow, Heads of the Valleys, Leicester, Liverpool, Manchester, Nottingham, Rhyl, Sheffield, Tyne and Wear and West London.

[6] Brent has now been broadened out to the West London City Strategy pilot.

[7] *Labour Force Survey*, Spring 2006.

7.19   However, delivering basic and employability skills can help people into work and ongoing training can be an important driver of increasing the number of people moving into work who are then able to stay in employment and progress. This can be done in part by helping to break down other barriers to work. Similarly, focusing on economically-valuable skills, as discussed in Chapter 3, can improve the employment and progression outcomes from gaining skills.

Recent progress   **7.20**   The recent introduction of the New Deal for Skills has aimed to ensure that people who are out of work get access to the training and support they need to find and stay in work. Skills Coaches, contracted by the LSC, provide an intensive, voluntary skills advice and guidance service for low skilled Jobcentre Plus customers in 19 pilot districts. In 5 Jobcentre Plus pilot districts, long-term claimants for whom skills are a key barrier to work are able to access a full-time Learning Option. The Employment Retention and Advancement (ERA) project is testing different ways of supporting people in work. Alongside financial incentives to encourage retention in work, ERA is testing the effectiveness of continued support, for up to 33 months, from a dedicated Advancement Support Adviser. The interim report will be available next year.

7.21   The Review has concluded that people need an integrated employment and skills service, building on progress to date, to ensure they receive the help they need to get on in work today, and an end to the current fragmentation. This builds on the conclusions of the recent Harker Review of child poverty, which found that '*to thrive in today's rapidly changing labour market, parents need guidance, support and skills to progress in work. A system which encourages parents to take any job rather than one that offers them good long-term prospects, or leads to parents 'cycling' between having a job and being out of work, is neither efficient nor effective in tackling child poverty*'.[8]

7.22   Such integration, as the Harker Review concluded, will contribute to reductions in child poverty. There is an urgent need to simplify the system and ensure it is better focused on the long-term, as well as short-term, needs of people and employers. To ensure that services are effectively focused on helping people succeed in the modern labour market, employers need a clearer point to input their views to ensure that services are delivering work ready people. The following sections set out the Review's recommendations.

INSTITUTIONAL REFORM

7.23   The Review has considered whether reforms to institutional structures would deliver a more integrated service for people. Chart 7.1 showed how the delivery of skills and employment services are separate and fragmented at national, regional and local level. This split accountability, contracting and delivery has contributed to individuals receiving a fragmented service.

Agency   **7.24**   Institutional change in England could take place at the agency level, between all or
structures   some parts of the LSC and Jobcentre Plus. There are clearly some overlaps between the responsibilities of the two bodies. Both, for example, commission a range of services, often from the same provider. However, full merger would create an immensely large organisation with responsibilities ranging from commissioning training from FE colleges to processing benefit claims. The risk is that such an organisation would be too unwieldy to manage and be two organisations under one roof, rather than a single entity. The fact that the LSC operates only in England while Jobcentre Plus is GB-wide is another complicating factor.

---

[8] *Delivering on child poverty: What would it take?*, Harker, DWP, 2006.

Departmental structures 7.25 The Review has also considered Departmental structures. The current DfES and DWP were formed in 2001, from the previous Department for Education and Employment (DfEE) and Department for Social Security (DSS). This was followed by the creation of Jobcentre Plus, which brought together the Benefits Agency, an agency of the DSS, and the Employment Service, an agency of the DfEE.

7.26 People did not have an integrated service when the DfEE existed: the current fragmentation has not been created by the separation of employment and education at Departmental level. Rather, it results from the objectives and incentives that each part of the system faces. In addition, separating skills from education, to create a Department for Work and Skills akin to the previous DfEE, would create significant problems of its own. While the divide between work and skills would have been eased, new ones would be created.

7.27 Recommending national institutional change would not necessarily deliver an integrated service for people. The Review's conclusion is that much can be achieved through changing the objectives that each part of the system faces, altering the policy they deliver and ensuring stretching scrutiny through local institutional rationalisation – making the current system work.

Reviewing arrangements 7.28 However, it is possible that this conclusion may change in the light of experience of trying to build an integrated service using the current structures. **The Review recommends the Commission for Employment and Skills report in 2010 on whether more radical structural change is required to deliver an integrated service.**

An Integrated Service

7.29 An integrated service would ensure people receive the support they need, including skills improvements, to find work. It would ensure that people do not have support cut off when they move into work, but are instead supported to stay in work and progress, building a seamless service for jobs and progression. This is essential to ensure people have the support they need to build economic security in the changing global economy.

Prize from an integrated service 7.30 The benefits of achieving this would be great. Ensuring that lone parents and those with disabilities and health problems get the full range of support they need to stay in work, including training, will contribute significantly to the Government's target of a 70 per cent lone parent employment rate and reducing the number of IB claimants by 1 million. It will also contribute to reductions in child poverty: the best way out of poverty is through sustainable work. In turn, ensuring that those at risk of cycling between welfare and work or becoming trapped in low paid work get the full range of in-work support they need, will aid progression and social mobility. This will have a positive impact on their children's lives: the life chances of children are closely related to the income, attainment and aspirations of their parents.

7.31 The Review has identified four key areas for reform to achieve an integrated service, realising the prize of increased employment and progression for disadvantaged groups, building on the reforms to the skills system set out in earlier chapters:

- better support for sustainable employment and progression;

- integrated front-line delivery of services;

- integrated objective of sustainable employment and progression; and

- enabling effective employer input.

BETTER SUPPORT FOR SUSTAINABLE EMPLOYMENT AND PROGRESSION

7.32   Current employment and skills services aim to help people find work and progress in a range of ways. The way in which they do so is determined by the incentives they face. The current Welfare to Work policy framework focuses on interventions to help people into work as quickly as possible and does not assess the help people need to stay in work and progress. For example, the Jobseeker's Allowance regime is designed to move people into work as quickly as possible, but there is no follow-up support for those who lack basic skills or are at risk of returning to benefits, unless they fail to find work in the short-term.

7.33   As a result, at risk groups do not get the full range of support they need to get into and stay in work. Skills interventions are rarely used by Jobcentre Plus, particularly in the short-term, as most people find work quickly and employment targets are based on job entry, rather than longer-term retention and progression. Only 11 per cent of people with identified basic skills needs on benefits complete a basic skills qualification. The incentives of colleges and other skills providers are to ensure people complete full qualifications, rather than ensuring these improve people's employment and pay outcomes. There is a big divide in the support people receive as they move into work. The Welfare to Work system is disconnected from in-work support, such as Train to Gain in England.

7.34   The Review has concluded that the support available to help people move into work needs to be improved. Support must be joined up across the transition to work. In most cases, it is best left to trained PAs to determine how best to help people find and stay in work, with employment providers rewarded for the outcomes they achieve. Similarly, skills providers must find their own ways of engaging priority clients and working with employers, rather than being told how to do so by planners.

Welfare to Work   **7.35**   To better support people to find and stay in work, the menu of support, including skills, that PAs access to help clients and the requirements benefit claimants face must be improved. In particular, across the UK, the Review recommends:

- a new programme to screen all benefit claimants for basic skills needs. This screening is currently done at the six month point of a claim. The Review recommends that all new claimants receive a light-touch screening when they claim benefit, with the results informing their 'Back to Work' plan;

- more help for people to improve their basic skills without delaying their return to work. All new claimants with a basic skills need should be referred to training once they move into work, or beforehand if their PA thinks this will significantly aid their return to work. Jobseekers who fail to find work within six months should be required to participate in basic skills training, alongside their job search requirements;

- improved support for people returning to benefits. The Government should consider requiring people cycling between welfare and work to have a full Skills Health Check, which would be acted on in their 'Back to Work' plan; and

- improving the quality of training. The Review recommends that all claimants for whom training is considered an appropriate option should access this training through a Learner Account that they can use at a range of accredited training providers.

Better identifying basic skills needs

7.36   For people to be effectively helped into work, their needs must first be properly identified. The Review has found that too many people do not have their basic skills needs identified. Basic skill needs among benefit claimants are more than double the national average. 38 per cent of claimants were without functional literacy skills and 45 per cent lacked functional numeracy skills. Similar proportions were also found for people with health problems. For some people, these problems can create major barriers to finding work. Those unable to read a job advert and fill in an application form are less likely to find work, stay in work or progress than those who can. The employment rate for those with basic skills needs is less than one half the UK average.

Current help   **7.37**   Measures have been introduced to help identify people for whom basic skills problems are a barrier to work. JSA claimants who remain on benefits for more than 6 months have a 'Fast Track' screening at the 6 month Restart interview, administered by their PA. This point was chosen to avoid focusing resources on those who would have got into work anyway, as two thirds of people leave JSA within the first 6 months of their claim. People claiming other benefits have a similar screen during their Work Focused Interview. In 2005-06, Jobcentre Plus planned to undertake around 1.5 million basic skills screenings, 0.5 million for those on JSA and 1 million for claimants of other benefits.

7.38   The Review recommends a much fuller role for the benefit system in tackling basic skills problems. The Review recommends that all benefit claimants be screened at the start of their claim, with new benefit claims and Work Focused Interviews becoming the trigger for a basic skills screening. Contact with the benefit system is a key opportunity to engage with people with low skills. Screening every new JSA claimant, will help to screen around two million people more each year: a significant proportion of the low skilled. As a consequence, those for whom basic skills needs are a barrier to work can be helped early. Those who find work in any case, can be helped to improve their skills in work.

Combining basic skills improvements and work

The current situation   **7.39**   People whose basic skills problems are seen as a barrier to finding a job by Jobcentre Plus PAs should be referred to training. There are currently two main types of provision. Basic Employability Training (BET) is available for those with the most severe need and can last up to 26 weeks. Short Intensive Basic Skills (SIBS) provides help for those with moderate literacy or numeracy needs, and can last for 8 weeks. The current system too often forces a choice between job search and skills improvements.

7.40   Recent pilots estimated the impact of incentives and sanctions for benefit claimants to improve their basic skills. They showed that mandating claimants to attend basic skills training has a small positive impact on attendance and completion.[9] The evaluation did not measure the long-term employment impact of such measures. There is some evidence that helping people improve their basic skills increases their long-term chances of finding work. After 40 months, there was a 5 per cent increase in employment outcomes for BET participants.[10] BET participation results in an improvement in the employment rates for participants of around three percentage points.[11] DWP have not collected data on progression and data on retention is limited. Poor referral, lack of incentives and lack of short-term

---

[9] *Evaluation of basic skills mandatory training pilot: Synthesis report*, DWP research report 385, 2006.

[10] *The longer term outcomes of work-based learning for adults: Evidence from administrative data*, Speckesser and Bewley, Policy Studies Institute, 2006.

[11] *The longer term outcomes of work-based learning for adults: evidence from administrative data*, Speckesser and Bewley, Policy Studies Institute, 2006.

employment impact, means that only 11 per cent of claimants identified as having a basic skills need go on to complete a basic skills qualification.

7.41   As a result of these evaluations, from September 2006 Jobcentre Plus customers will be able to access a new basic skills programme from the LSC. Jobcentre Plus is also working with the LSC on a new basic skills product for Jobcentre Plus customers to be introduced in August 2007. This will combine employability and skills acquisition.

7.42   It is critical to avoid delaying people's return to work. At present, once people move into work, there is no follow up support or encouragement to take up the training needed to reduce the risk of returning to benefits. The average time taken to complete a basic skills course is around 60 hours and they can be delivered part-time to fit around work and job search. There is no reason for this false choice: the job search requirement could be combined with referrals to training once people enter work, or with part-time skills improvements for those who fail to find work in the early stages of job search.

Integrating basic   **7.43**   The Review recommends that people claiming JSA whose basic skills needs are a key
skills   barrier to work should have part-time basic skills improvements included in their action
improvements   plans, alongside actions to find work. For people identified with a need, support should be offered in a way that best suits their job seeking or work status, and in a way that will not encourage people to remain on benefits simply in order to start or complete their training. The Review recommends:

- new JSA claimants with basic skills needs should be referred to training when they have found work, or before if their PA finds that basic skills needs are the key barrier to work. Referring claimants to training when they have found work will be the responsibility of Jobcentre Plus PAs, working with Train to Gain brokers in England;

- for people with basic skills needs who remain on JSA after six months, there is a strong case for making basic skills training compulsory. The Government should review whether participation should be mandatory for all jobseekers with basic skills needs who remain on benefits at six months; and

- to help address basic skills problems for disadvantaged groups, basic skills improvements should be more fully integrated into support such as Pathways to Work for people with health problems and disabilities and the New Deal for lone parents (NDLP).

7.44   These measures will ensure that people get help tailored to their needs. People whose basic skills needs prevent them from finding work will receive help and support to improve their basic skills, alongside action to find work. Where basic skills are not an immediate barrier to finding work, their basic skills needs will be properly diagnosed and they will be referred to provision that is flexibly tailored to their new job. This will help significant numbers of people improve their basic skills each year, contributing to increased employment among disadvantaged groups and improved retention as well as reduced child poverty. Jobcentre Plus and training providers should work as far as they can to ensure as many people as possible referred to basic skills courses by their PA complete their course.

People returning to benefits

7.45   Around two thirds of all JSA claims each year are repeat claims, some 1.6 million claims. While some degree of cycling is inevitable in a well-functioning labour market, it is important to ensure that all claimants receive effective support to find and stay in work. Those most at risk of being trapped in worklessness and most at risk of returning to benefits need targeted help.

7.46   At present, repeat claimants are treated in the same way as new claimants. Under the Review's recommendations above, they will have their basic skills needs identified at the start of their first claim. Additional support for some of this group, particularly those making multiple claims, could help them find work more quickly or stay in work for longer. However, those that would benefit most may be hard to identify.

Extra help for people making repeat claims   **7.47**   The Review recommends that people making repeat claims get fuller support to find and stay in employment. The Government should consider whether all claimants making multiple benefit claims in a given period, or out of work for a certain proportion of the previous year, should get extra support. This could include a full Skills Health Check, wider than the basic skills screening. This should be acted on in their Back to Work plan. The Government should also consider whether people with an identified basic skill need who make multiple benefit claims in a given period should be required to improve their basic skills earlier in their claim than the six month period recommended above.

Improving the quality of training

7.48   People will only benefit from training if it is high quality and work focused. The poor quality of basic skills provision, for example, is a key driver of the fact that only 11 per cent of those with identified basic skills needs go on to complete a basic skills qualification. There has been a range of attempts to ensure that training for benefit claimants is high quality and work focused. These have often focused on engaging employers and linking jobs available to specific training as discussed in Box 7.2.

> ### Box 7.2: Linking employers and Welfare to Work
>
> At the local level, employment services such as Jobcentre Plus often work closely with employers to attempt to better match benefit claimants with the jobs available. There have also been a number of initiatives that aim to do this in a systematic way.
>
> The National Employer Panel (NEP) has developed ten Employer Coalitions, each based in and around a major city across the UK. These engage local businesses in the development and promotion of the New Deal and other Welfare to Work programmes. A prominent local business leader chairs each Coalition, which form a network of local employer groups with well over 1,000 members. Each Coalition is focused on: engaging local firms in the design and delivery of Welfare to Work programmes; advising Jobcentre Plus on how to enhance the performance of Welfare to Work and acting as a catalyst for innovation and excellence.
>
> Fair Cities pilots were established in 2005 in Birmingham, Bradford and Brent. The pilots aim to increase the number of disadvantaged ethnic minority residents who gain steady work, and so help reduce the employment gap for ethnic minority groups. The fundamental principle underpinning Fair Cities is the demand-led approach, which seeks to engage them in the design and delivery of customised training for workless residents.
>
> The Ambition pilots were set up in 2002 to test a demand-led approach to job preparation and training. Pilots were established in a number of sectors, including retail, energy, and construction, with integrated packages of training and work experience, designed in close consultation with employers to meet their specific entry requirements. There is evidence to suggest that the offer of a good job engaged some disaffected customers who had previously not responded well to mainstream provision.[a]
>
> [a] *Ambition stocktake report: An interim report on the development and progress of the Ambition initatives*, National Employment Panel, 2004.

7.49   Chapter 4 set out recommendations to improve the quality and economic value of training by making adult vocational skills funding in England demand-led through Train to Gain and Learner Accounts. This will ensure that providers only receive funding if they attract individuals and employers in and meet their needs flexibly. Exactly the same argument applies for benefit claimants being recommended training by their Jobcentre Plus PA. All benefit claimants referred to training should access this training through a Learner Account which they can use at any provider accredited by the LSC. By ensuring that they access training through a Learner Account, rather than centralised contracting, the quality of training and the times and ways it is delivered will be improved.

FRONT-LINE DELIVERY

7.50   In the modern labour market, people will need to update their skills more often as they change jobs, adapt to new technology and working lives lengthen. They need integrated, work-focused advice on how to do this. At present, Jobcentre Plus is the main source of help and advice on finding a job for those on benefits. A range of providers in England, from a national network of nextstep centres to the learndirect phone line and website, offers advice on improving skills. There is some cross-referral between services. For example, Jobcentre Plus refer around 50,000 people to learndirect each year. Skills Coaches operate in Jobcentres in 19 pilot areas, through the New Deal for Skills. Further details on the provision of skills advice across the UK can be found in Chapter 6.

7.5I   As Chapter 6 showed, the current system for providing skills and employment advice is confusing and fragmented. Skills advice is often provided out of the context of building a career. Employment advice focuses on getting a job rather than progression paths. Very often this support is not joined up so that people can get advice on getting into work and progressing. As a consequence, people do not know where to go for advice on how to get on in work, and are only offered support in organisational 'silos'. In some other countries, support is more joined up. Box 7.3 gives details of the approach adopted in the USA.

Box 7.3: One stop shops in the USA

The United States has experimented with aggregating skills and unemployment agencies into 'One Stop Centres'. These centres were established following the Workforce Investment Act of 1998. The Centres deal with employment, training, and rehabilitation. They integrate the local functions of the federal agencies of Education, Labour, and Health and Human Services. This is intended to reduce complexity for the unskilled and unemployed.

The 'One Stop Centres' are physical locations that any citizen can access for free. The resources available at these centres include labour market information; job coaching for youths; retraining for seniors; displaced worker services; computer and telephone access for job seekers; and job training. Most of these services are entirely free for users, and training is provided free to low-income workers, the recently unemployed, the disabled, and individuals who speak a foreign language. In most cases, citizens are provided with an 'Individual Training Account', which they use to purchase training at the One Stop Centres.

The physical locations are accompanied by an internet backbone, known as 'America's Career Kit'. This service consists of three websites: 'America's job bank', which provides information on vacancies; 'America's Career InfoNet', which provides broader labour market information; and 'America's Learning eXchange', which provides information on training.

7.52   There are good examples of integration of services happening at the local level in the UK. The Review has seen several of these, summarised in Box 7.4. In Northern Ireland, the all-age careers service operates in a number of locations, including co-location with Jobs and Benefits Offices and Jobcentres.

> ## Box 7.4: Local examples of integrated support
>
> The Review has seen a number of local attempts to bring skills and employment advice together. The Training and Employment Advice Shop in Reading, for instance, provides residents with careers advice, job search facilities and a variety of training courses in one central location. It works in partnership with a number of organisations, including Reading Council, Jobcentre Plus, Business Link and local colleges and engages in several outreach activities, providing the same information and advice services in local community venues.
>
> Pertemps, a Working Neighbourhoods pilot in Birmingham, operates a similar model, with employment advisors working alongside a learndirect training centre. Individuals can also access advice on financial issues and other specialist support services.
>
> King's Cross Working caters specifically for the construction industry. Training, job brokerage and support services are delivered in a single, dedicated centre in the middle of one of the largest construction sites in London.
>
> In Scotland, the Working Neighbourhood Pilot in Glasgow, run by Working Links, specialises in delivering sustainable employment to the local community. Located in the heart of the community, it engages the hard to reach through outreach activities and provides counselling services for both employers and workers throughout the first six months of employment.
>
> Support has been brought together in a number of other policy areas too. Sure Start brings together early education, childcare, health and family support. By 2008, up to 2,500 Children's Centres will help families with children under 5 get affordable childcare and early education.

7.53   This approach is generally considered successful. Co-locating services is more convenient for customers. It opens up easy access to both employment and careers advice to all benefit claimants, from the unemployed to lone parents and those with health problems and disabilities. It facilitates much closer cross-working between services. Co-location makes services simpler and easier to access for individuals, and facilitates joint and complementary working between services. As the labour market continues to change and working lives lengthen, people will increasingly need access to integrated advice on how to build their careers and update their skills.

The Review's recommendations: A new, universal adult careers service

A new, universal adult careers service

7.54   To meet the challenge of helping people in the modern labour market, Chapter 6 set out the Review's recommendation of a new universal adult careers service. This will provide labour market focused careers advice for all adults, in and out of work, in the UK. It will do this in a range of locations, including in the community, online and over the phone. This new careers service is at the heart of the Review's strategy for ensuring that people have the advice and support they need to succeed in the modern labour market.

One-stop shops **7.55** The Review recommends that the new adult careers service also be co-located with Jobcentre Plus and other providers of employment support, while also operating from other locations such as colleges. This will establish a nationwide network of one stop shops for employment and skills advice, building on best practice already seen across the UK and other countries. It will ensure that there is a high profile location that everyone seeking advice on improving their career or getting into work can go to. People who are out of work will have much greater and easier access to skills and careers advice than they do currently. As Chapter 6 set out, this should not be the only place people can get help, flexibility of delivery is key.

7.56 This network of one stop shops will, in England, involve the co-location of the new national careers service with employment services (both Jobcentre Plus and, where services are contracted out, private and third sector providers). The careers service will become the source of skills expertise for Jobcentre Plus. The Review recommends that the careers service provide skills diagnosis for workless people who need it in England, including those making repeat claims, with Jobcentre Plus referring claimants to it.

7.57 These one stop shops should not be the only source of skills and employment advice. As Chapter 6 set out, the new national careers service will be required to operate flexibly, reaching out to people in communities, shopping centres and other places, rather than having just one location. In Scotland, Wales and Northern Ireland, the Devolved Administrations should consider how best to integrate their careers services with employment services so that this approach can work across the UK.

OBJECTIVES AND INCENTIVES

7.58 At the heart of both employment and skills services are the objectives and incentives that those delivering them face. It is these objectives and incentives that drive the services that people receive. Getting these incentives right is a pre-requisite for delivering a joined up service for individuals.

Current objectives and incentives

7.59 The Review has found that current targets and incentives do not fully encourage a joined-up service for individuals. The focus on helping people get into work and stay there for 13 weeks means that the Welfare to Work system has no incentive to focus on the interventions and links with in – work support, including skills, that would improve job retention or progression. The focus of the skills system on qualification attainment has led to too little focus on the employment outcomes of those improving their skills and little focus on those with the greatest labour market disadvantage. The focus of each system on different, but closely related, goals has worked against the integrated approach advocated above.

Employment **7.60** The key employment objective of the Department for Work and Pensions (DWP) is to **objectives** increase the employment rate over the economic cycle. It has translated this into operational targets for Jobcentre Plus to help a certain number of people off benefits and into work each year, with a focus on disadvantaged groups. Private and third sector providers are rewarded for benefit off-flows and retention in work after 13 weeks. Jobcentre Plus also had a focus on retention after 13 weeks, but this has since been dropped.

7.61   As oot out above, while the employment rate is at historically and internationally high levels, large numbers of people make repeat claims for benefit. This group comprises around two thirds of Jobcentre Plus' JSA caseload. The Review has concluded that the focus of Jobcentre Plus on job entries and short-term retention draws PA's attention away from pre-work interventions that might improve the longer-term sustainability of employment, as well as creating little incentive to build links with in-work support that might improve retention and progression.

Skills objectives 7.62   The Government and Devolved Administrations have stretching targets to improve the skills of young people and adults across the UK, set out in Table 2.1. In England, these targets feed down into operational targets for the LSC to deliver a given number of qualification attainments at each level. The income of colleges largely depends on ensuring learners complete full qualifications. Training providers have little incentive to focus on those who need support the most to stay in work or to work with employment providers. Similar incentives operate in the rest of the UK.

7.63   The LSC is currently carrying out work to improve the availability of data in England on the employment and pay prospects of students as part of the development of the key performance indicators. However, at present, many colleges do not routinely collect and publicise the employment and pay prospects of their students in a systematic way. Being able to demonstrate that those completing a course have good pay and job prospects helps attract more students in and will be increasingly essential as the system becomes fully demand-led.

The Review's proposals: an integrated objective for all services

An integrated 7.64   The Review recommends that the objectives of the employment and skills systems
objective should be transformed into an integrated objective of sustainable employment and progression. This will be a major change for all Departments and agencies in the system, requiring them to work in fundamentally different ways. For this integrated objective to be delivered, it must be tangible and measurable. The Review recommends that DfES and DWP present their proposals for measuring the employment and pay prospects and progression of their customers in 2007.

7.65   This integrated objective must cascade down through the targets of Departments, as well as those of delivery agencies and front line workers, transforming the way they are rewarded, the way they work and the services they provide. Changing their incentives will lead front line workers and agencies to find the best ways to help people move into, stay in and progress in work. Each Department must measure the contribution of each of its agencies to the sustainable employment and progression of their customers. For example, the contribution of employment services will involve ensuring claimants have basic employability skills and building full and effective links with services such as Train to Gain, so that claimants are guaranteed proper support in work.

Departmental aims 7.66 The contribution of each Department is outlined in its Public Service Agreements (PSAs). The DfES should continue to be held accountable for improving skills and delivering qualifications through the new PSA framework, with the volumes set out in Chapter 3. In line with the commitments in the FE reform White Paper,[12] it should require skills providers to measure the employment and pay prospects of a representative sample of those completing courses over a three year period, similar to the approach already taken by some universities. The DWP should be held accountable through the PSA framework for improving the employment rate over the cycle. The Commission will monitor annually whether DfES skills policy and DWP employment policy is making a full contribution to sustained employment and progression.

Delivery incentives 7.67 The integrated objective of achieving sustainable employment and progression must cascade down into the incentives faced by the agencies and contracted providers of skills and employment services. Measuring the sustainability of employment and progression of benefit claimants and those improving their skills is the first step. The second step is to measure the contribution of each agency and provider to this sustainability and progression.

7.68 In practice, this means that Jobcentre Plus and others delivering Welfare to Work services should still be rewarded for getting people into work. However, they should be rewarded for retention in work for at least a year. Their contribution to supporting progression includes referrals to in-work support and delivery of basic employability skills. This will give providers strong incentives to help people improve their retention and progression, including through skills improvements. The Commisison will monitor whether Jobcentre Plus is making its full contribution to sustainable employment and progression.

7.69 Similarly, the income of colleges and learning providers in England should still rely on learners gaining full qualifications. Within the framework already being developed, providers should be required to track the job prospects and pay progression of a representative sample of those completing their courses, as some universities already do. This data should be published to enable people to make an informed choice about where to learn.

7.70 Colleges and the new adult careers service should be rewarded partly on the basis of these outcomes and for helping people move into work. This will give skills providers better incentives to help people translate skills improvements into improved pay and job prospects and to focus support on the disadvantaged and the workless. The Devolved Administrations should consider how to ensure colleges are rewarded for providing economically valuable skills in the rest of the UK.

ENABLING EFFECTIVE EMPLOYER INPUT

7.71 To ensure that local services are delivering an integrated service for individuals, they must be held to account for their delivery of this service. Effective employer input is vital to ensure that skills and employment services deliver economically valuable outcomes. The earlier sections showed the galaxy of initiatives that currently exists to do this. It showed the complexity that this creates, its over-reliance on planning rather than being demand-led and the fact that accountability for employment and skills services is as fragmented and separated as delivery of these services.

---

[12] *FE reform: Raising skills, improving life chances*, DfES, 2006.

7.72   There is an urgent need to simplify and rationalise so that employers are clear about where and how to engage with the system. An integrated service with a single objective should have an integrated accountability framework. The Review recommends an integrated accountability structure, giving employers a key role in ensuring that all parts of the system are working toward the shared objective.

National level   **7.73**   At the national level, the Commission for Employment and Skills will replace the National Employment Panel (NEP) and SSDA across the UK, and the Skills Alliance and employer voice functions of the LSC in England. It will be a key driver for integrating employment and skills services, ensuring they work together to meet the needs of the economy, employers and individuals. It will be responsible, at the national level, for recommending improvements to all parts of the skills and employment systems, from Departments to agencies, to ensure they work toward the integrated objective the Review recommends. See Chapter 4 for more details.

Local level   **7.74**   At present, there is a range of vehicles that work to deliver a more joined-up approach below national level and ensure the input of employers. These include Regional Skills Partnerships, city strategy Pathfinder partnerships and Work and Skills Boards being developed in the big cities. The large number of bodies and initiatives, often with overlapping responsibilities and priorities, confuses employers, leaving them unsure how and where they can influence the system. In addition, too many of the bodies relating to skills are focused on planning provision, whereas, as Chapter 4 set out, demand-led approaches work far better.

7.75   The recent DCLG White Paper noted that there *'may be more than one way to tackle the challenge of joining up employment and skills'* but suggested the Core Cities in particular could make a real difference.[13] It concluded that Skills and Employment Boards provide a *'more strategic approach to employer engagement, skills and employment.'* Employment and Skills Boards are already developing, through local initiative, in a number of cities. In London, the Mayor's new board will set the strategic direction for adult skills for a single London LSC, replacing the previous local LSCs, and taking on the role of the RSP.

7.76   The Review supports this approach and recommends the licensing by the Commission of a network of Employment and Skills Boards (ESBs), based on the NEP Employer Coalitions and existing initiatives. The Boards will have two main non-executive roles, mirroring those of the Commission:

- monitoring the local labour market. The Boards will monitor local skills, productivity and employment. They will articulate the needs of local employers, recommend improvements to the delivery of the integrated employment and skills service and have funding to innovate in helping disadvantaged groups back to work; and

- raising employer engagement. The Boards will engage with local employers to raise their investment in skills and engagement with Welfare to Work. This could include brokering agreements between employers and providers.

7.77   The Review recommends a flexible approach to the licensing of ESBs, using existing arrangements, such as NEP Employer Coalitions, where appropriate. It will be important to avoid a 'one size fits all' approach. Licensing should ensure that the geography of the Boards fits with the conclusions of the forthcoming HM Treasury review of sub-national governance.

---

[13] *Strong and Prosperous Communities, the Local Government White Paper*, DCLG, 2006. The Core Cities are: Birmingham, Bristol, Leeds, Liverpool, Manchester, Newcastle, Nottingham and Sheffield.

7.78   Adopting this flexible approach will give significant scope for simplifying the current complex arrangements. The criteria for licensing could include:

- leadership by eminent local employers, with trades unions and independent representation;

- a large enough scale to be recognised as a functional economic area, while sufficiently local to allow effective scrutiny of services; and

- agreement that the Board must operate within the national framework for employment and skills.

7.79   It is important that providers of services and other partners, such as LAs, also have opportunities to ensure they work in an integrated way and support disadvantaged groups. There is a range of existing structures that provide for this and Boards will work with these and recommend improvements.

CONCLUSION

7.80   The UK's overall employment rate is high by both international and historic standards. This is, in part, the result of a successful Welfare to Work programme for workless people that successfully gets people into work. The UK's skills profile is improving as a result of a skills system focused on people getting full qualifications.

7.81   The Review has found that too many people find it difficult to get into work and to stay in employment and progress. These problems are most acute among the low skilled. Weaknesses in the Welfare to Work and skills systems, coupled with disjoints between them, are contributing to these problems and meaning people do not get the full range of support they need to get on at work.

7.82   The Review recommends an integrated employment and skills service that delivers the full range of support that people need in the modern labour market. This service will ensure people have integrated advice on skills and employment.

7.83   In particular, the Review recommends that all benefit claimants be screened for basic skills needs at the start of their claim. Where basic skills needs are a barrier to work, they will be referred to part-time basic skills improvements, alongside activity to find work. Where they find work, they will be referred to skills development in work, through Train to Gain in England. JSA claimants with basic skills needs who remain out of work for more than six months will be required to improve their basic skills, alongside action to find work. The Review also recommends fuller support for those who find it difficult to stay in work. The Government should consider a full Skills Health Check for those who find it most difficult to stay in work with the results shaping their Back to Work plan. These reforms will ensure that skills help is fully integrated with help to find a job.

7.84   To ensure that everyone can get the advice they need to succeed in the modern labour market, the Review recommends a national careers service in England, detailed in Chapter 6. This should provide labour market focused advice. It should operate in a number of locations, including co-location with Jobcentre Plus and employment advice, creating a nationwide network of one-stop shops.

7.85   In this way, employment support will be more fully integrated with skills support, building a welfare system prepared for the challenges of the new century. People will have easy access to the help and advice they need to succeed in a modern labour market being reshaped by global economic changes.

SUMMARY OF RECOMMENDATIONS

8.1   In 2004, following the publication of *Skills in the global economy* alongside the Pre-Budget Report, Sandy Leitch, a former chief executive of Zurich Financial Services and chairman of the National Employment Panel, was commissioned by the Government to lead an independent review of skills.

8.2   The Chancellor of the Exchequer and the Secretary of State for Education and Skills commissioned the Leitch Review to identify the UK's optimal skills mix in 2020 to maximise economic growth, productivity and social justice, and to consider the policy implications of achieving the level of change required.

8.3   In addition, at Budget 2006 the Chancellor asked the Review to report specifically on *'how skills and employment services can complement each other even more effectively in supporting labour market flexibility, better employment outcomes and greater progression to productive and sustainable jobs for those with skill needs.'*

8.4   The Review's main recommendations are set out below, with subsidiary recommendations for implementation.

MAKING THE UK A WORLD LEADER IN SKILLS

Increasing attainments

8.5   The Review recommends a new ambition to achieve world class skills. Achieving world class skills will require the UK to commit to achieving by 2020:[1]

- 95 per cent of adults to have the basic skills of functional literacy and numeracy up from 85 per cent literacy and 79 per cent numeracy in 2005; more than trebling projected rates of improvement to achieve a total of 7.4 million adult attainments over the period;

- exceeding 90 per cent of the adult population qualified to at least Level 2, with a commitment to achieving world class levels as soon as feasible, currently projected to be 95 per cent. An increase from 70 per cent today; a total of up to 5.7 million adult attainments over the period;

- shifting the balance of intermediate skills from Level 2 to Level 3. Improving the esteem, quantity and quality of intermediate skills. Boosting the number of Apprentices in the UK to 500,000; a total of 4 million adult attainments over the period; and

- world class high skills, with a commitment to exceed 40 per cent of the adult population to be qualified to Level 4 or above. Widening the drive to improve the UK's high skills to encompass the whole working-age population, including preparing young adults for their working lives; a total of 5.5 million attainments over the period.

Delivering world class skills

8.6   If the UK wants world class skills, it needs world class attainment among young people. Despite significant improvements in schools, there is further to go to ensure all young people leave school with the platform of skills they need in the modern labour market.

---

[1] Adults means age 19 to State Pension age.

8.7 More than 70 per cent of the 2020 working age population are already over the age of 16. As the global economy changes and working lives lengthen, adults will increasingly need to update their skills in the work place.

A new partnership 8.8 Since 1945 debate has polarised around whether the Government needs to regulate to increase employer investment in training. The Review recommends a new partnership approach, building on the success of recent initiatives to build a more demand-led system, meeting the new challenges the UK faces through common action. In practice, this means:

- **Government,** investing more, focusing on the least skilled. Ensuring that the education system delivers a highly-skilled flow into the workforce. Creating a framework to ensure employers and individuals drive the skills system to deliver economically valuable skills. Being prepared to act on market failures, targeting help where it is most needed. Regulate if necessary and with care to reach the UK's skills ambitions;

- **employers,** to increase their investment in skills to impact productivity, wherever possible increasing investment in portable accredited training. Ensuring the skills system delivers economically valuable skills by effectively influencing the system. Pledging to support their low-skilled employees to reach at least a first full Level 2. Introducing sectoral measures, such as levies, where a majority of employers in the sector agree; and

- **individuals,** raising their aspirations and awareness. Demanding more of their employers. Investing more in their own skills development.

A DEMAND-LED SYSTEM

Demand-led funding 8.9 The Review recommends a simplified demand-led system with employers and individuals having a strong and coherent voice. **The Review recommends that all publicly funded, adult vocational skills in England, apart from community learning, go through demand-led routes by 2010.** This means all adult skills funding should be routed through Train to Gain and Learner Accounts by 2010. The switch to demand-led funding and end to the supply-side planning of adult skills provision fundamentally changes the role planning bodies, such as the LSC, which will require further significant streamlining.

8.10 The Review recommends that a portion of higher education funding for vocational courses, currently administered through HEFCE in England, be delivered through a similar demand-led mechanism as Train to Gain. This should use government funding to lever in greater investment by employers at Level 4 and Level 5. The Devolved Administrations should consider how best to ensure that provision is effectively led by the needs of employers and individuals.

Strengthening employer voice 8.11 The Review recommends strengthening the voice of employers through the creation of a single, employer-led Commission for Employment and Skills to deliver leadership and influence within a national framework of individual rights and responsibilities. The Commission will replace the SSDA and NEP across the UK. In England, the Commission will also replace the Skills Alliance.

Increasing employer engagement

8.12   The Review recommends a new, clearer remit for Sector Skills Councils, focused on:

- raising employer engagement, demand and investment;

- lead role in vocational qualifications;

- lead role in collating and communicating sectoral labour market data; and

- considering collective measures.

Economically valuable qualifications

8.13   The Review has developed recommendations to ensure qualifications deliver economic value. The Review recommends that Sector Skills Councils continue to lead in developing National Occupational Standards, the building blocks of qualifications. It recommends that SSCs are also placed in charge of a simplified process of developing qualifications that follows this.

8.14   Sector Skills Councils should be responsible for approving qualifications after their development by examining boards or lead bodies, rather than the QCA. SSCs will be able to approve qualifications developed by an organisation, including education institutions and employers, if these meet the required standards.

8.15   For vocational qualifications, only those approved by SSCs should qualify for public funding. This would apply to funding for work based learning qualifications such as NVQs, including Levels 4 and 5, through the LSC. SSCs should develop a short list of such qualifications, with a very significant reduction in the overall number, by 2008. Arrangements in Wales, Scotland and Northern Ireland should be developed by the Devolved Administrations.

EMPLOYER ENGAGEMENT IN SKILLS

8.16   Achieving world class skills will require shared action between employers and the Government. The Review recommends a partnership to drive increased attainment at each level and better use of skills.

Management and leadership

8.17   To further improve the UK's management and leadership, the Review recommends that Sector Skills Councils drive up employer investment in these skills by employers. The Review recommends that the Leadership and Management programme be extended to firms with between 10 and 20 employees, so that smaller firms are able to access its help and grow.

8.18   It is vital that current business support is simplified and strengthened. Skills advice must be integrated as part of this wider system of support. As Train To Gain continues to roll out, the National Employer Service should be expanded to provide a more effective advisory and brokerage service to larger firms.

Training low-skilled employees

8.19   The Review recommends a major campaign to encourage all employers in the UK to make a skills pledge that every employee be enabled to gain basic skills and a first full Level 2 equivalent qualification.

8.20   In 2010, the Government and the Commission should review progress in the light of take-up and employer delivery on their "Pledges". If the improvement rate is insufficient, Government should introduce a statutory entitlement to workplace training for individuals without a full Level 2 qualification or equivalent. The entitlement will need to be carefully designed so that it minimises bureaucracy and avoids being overly prescriptive. It must be designed in consultation with employers and trades unions.

Investment in higher skill levels

8.21   The Review recommends that employers drive up attainment of intermediate and high skills, including in Apprenticeships, led by SSCs and skills brokers. As with qualifications, SSCs should control the content of Apprenticeships and set attainment targets by sector. This should lead to a boosting in the number of Apprenticeships in the UK to 500,000 a year by 2020.

8.22   The Review recommends widening the focus of HE targets to encompass both young people and adults via workplace delivery. This will dramatically improve engagement between HE and employers.

EMBEDDING A CULTURE OF LEARNING

8.23   The Review recommends a new offer to adults to help further embed a culture of learning across the country, ensuring everyone gets the help they need to get on in life: raising awareness and aspiration; making informed choices; increasing choice; and ensuring individuals can afford to learn.

Raising aspirations and awareness

8.24   The Review has developed fresh recommendations to raise awareness and aspiration among adults across society. At the heart of these is a new universal careers service for England, bringing together current separate sources of advice. The Review recommends that this service operate under the already successful and well-known learndirect brand.

8.25   This service will be charged with raising aspiration and awareness of the importance and benefits of learning, particularly among those that have missed out in the past. It will lead a sustained national campaign to promote skills development among groups that would not normally consider learning. The Review recommends that all adults should be entitled to a free 'Skills Health Check', building on the success of a similar approach in Sweden, that would identify an individual's skill needs and strengths.

Improving choice

8.26   To improve individuals choice and control, the Review recommends that all adult further education funding for individuals in England, including the current Level 2 entitlement, be channelled through Learner Accounts by 2010. Over time, the Government should consider rolling other forms of financial support into these accounts, such as the learner support discussed in the following section and any childcare support.

Financial support

8.27   The Review recommends a new system of financial support, based on the principle of transparency and building on best practice elsewhere:

- clear and transparent financial support for those considering skills development as well as for existing learners; and

- greater use of Career Development Loans particularly for those looking to progress to intermediate level and beyond.

8.28   The Review recommends that a Skills Development Fund (SDF) replace the LSF. Based on clear eligibility criteria, advisers should use this fund flexibly to tackle the immediate financial barriers to learning that potential and current learners face.

INTEGRATING EMPLOYMENT AND SKILLS

8.29 The Review recommends a new integrated employment and skills service to help people meet the challenges of the modern labour market. To ensure people can access an integrated employment and skills service, the Review recommends:

- a new programme to help benefit claimants with basic skills problems. Including a new programme to screen all benefit claimants, and more help to improve their basic skills;

- a new universal adult careers service, providing labour market focused careers advice for all adults. The new careers service will deliver advice in a range of locations, including co-location with Jobcentre Plus, drawing on Jobcentre Plus information and services, creating a national network of one stop shops for careers and employment advice;

- a new integrated objective for employment and skills services of sustainable employment and progression. Meeting this will require all involved in such services, from Departments, the LSC and Jobcentre Plus, to front line staff and colleges, to focus on people's long-term, as well as short-term, prospects; and

- a network of employer-led Employment and Skills Boards to give employers a central role in recommending improvements to local services, mirroring the national role of the Commission for Employment and Skills. The Boards will work to ensure that local services meet employer needs and the workless are equipped to access work.

NEXT STEPS

8.30 This policy framework will deliver world class skills, given the right investment and delivery reform. However, this is not a detailed blueprint for implementation. Government should now consider these recommendations and decide the next steps of the journey.

8.31 The Devolved Administrations in Northern Ireland, Scotland and Wales should now consider the Review's recommended policy framework in the context of differing circumstances in those countries and their contribution for delivering world class, economically valuable skills.

A BACKGROUND TO THE REVIEW

A.1   In 2004, following the publication of *Skills in the global economy* alongside the Pre-Budget Report, Sandy Leitch, a former Chief Executive of Zurich Financial Services and chairman of the National Employment Panel, was commissioned by the Government to lead an independent review of skills.[1]

A.2   The Chancellor of the Exchequer and the Secretary of State for Education and Skills commissioned the Leitch Review to identify the UK's optimal skills mix in 2020 to maximise economic growth, productivity and social justice, and to consider the policy implications of achieving the level of change required.

A.3   In particular, the Review was asked to:

- examine the UK's optimum skills mix in order to maximise economic growth and productivity by 2020; and

- consider the different trajectories of skill levels the UK might pursue.

A.4   The Review team is composed of officials from both HM Treasury and the Department for Education and Skills, with an advisory member from the Sector Skills Development Agency. The Review's UK-wide remit has also ensured close co-operation with officials in the Scottish Executive and also work with the other devolved administrations to ensure proper reflection of differences in data and policy.

A.5   The Review has worked with key stakeholders, including those in the Government, the Departments, agencies and education and training providers with a remit to improve the UK's skills, businesses and trades unions. The Leitch Review would like to thank of all these organisations for their help and support.

A.6   The Review has drawn on evidence from a wide variety of sources. A Call for Evidence was sent to over 250 organisations, including employers and their representatives, unions and organisations providing education and training. Responses were also received through the Review's website. For more information on the Call for Evidence, please see Annex B of the Review's interim report.

A.7   *Skills in the UK: the long-term challenge*, published alongside the 2005 Pre-Budget Report, sets out the Review's interim analysis. It committed the Review to addressing three key issues:

- the skills profile that the UK should aim to achieve in 2020 to drive growth, productivity and social justice over the longer-term;

- the appropriate balance of responsibility between the Government, employers and individuals for the action required to meet this level of change; and

- the policy framework required to support this.

A.8   The Review has spent the time since publication of the interim report working closely with a range of stakeholders in order to address these issues. This report contains its final conclusions and is published alongside the 2006 Pre-Budget Report.

---

[1] *Skills in the global economy*, HM Treasury, 2004.

BIBLIOGRAPHY

Ali, (2005), Inspection report, Learndirect advice

Amsden, (1989), Asia's next giant: South Korea and late industrialisation

Ashton and Sung, (2006), Lessons from abroad: developing sector based approaches to skills, Sector Skills Development Agency

Barclays Bank, (2001), in Parkinson et al, (2004) Urban Renaissance of EU non-capital cities

Bell, Burriel-Llombart and Jones, Bank of England Working Paper 280, (2005), A quality-adjusted labour input series for the United Kingdom (1975-2002)

Blanden and Gregg, Oxford Review of Economic Policy, 2, 245-263, (2004), Family income and educational attainment: A review of approaches and evidence for Britain

Blanden, Gregg and Machin, CEP, London School of Economics, (2005), Intergenerational mobility in Europe and North America.

Blanden, Gregg and Machin, (2005), Intergenerational Mobility in Europe and North America

Blenkinsop et al, (2006), How do young people make choices at 14 and 16?

Bloom, Dorgan, Dowdy, van Reenan, Rippin, (2005),Management practices across firms and nations, LSE-Mckinsey

Carey, Low and Hansbro, ONS, (1997), Adult literacy in Britain

Cassen and Mavrotas, (1997), Education and training for manufacturing development in Godfrey (ed), Skill development for international competitiveness, Institute of Development Studies, University of Sussex

Chartered Institute of Personal Development, (2006), Recruitment, retention and turnover study

Confederation of British Industry, (2006), Employer Trends Survey

Confederation of British Industry, (2006), The importance of leadership and management skills to employers – Survey evidence

Corak (ed), (2004), Generational income mobility in North America and Europe, Cambridge University Press

Dearden et al, (2004), An in-depth analysis of the returns to National Vocational Qualifications obtained at Level 2, CEE

Dearden, Reed and van Reenan, Institute for Fiscal Studies (2000), Who gains when workers train? Training and corporate productivity in a panel of British industries

Dearden, Reed and van Reenan, (2005), The impact of training on productivity and wages: evidence from British panel data

Department for Education and Skills, (2002), National Adult Learning Survey

Department for Education and Skills, (2003), Education and Skills: The economic benefit

Department for Education and Skills, (2003), Skills for life survey

Department for Education and Skills, (2003), The future of higher education

Department for Education and Skills, (2005), White Paper, Skills: getting on in business, getting on at work

Department for Education and Skills, (2006), Intermediate impacts of advice and guidance

Department for Education and Skills, (2006), Departmental Report

Department of Health, (2005), Independence, well-being and choice: Our vision for the future of social care for adults in England

Department of Work and Pensions, (2006), The impact of free movement of workers from Central and Eastern Europe on the UK labour market

Department for Communities and Local Government, (2006), Strong and prosperous communities, the Local Government White Paper

Dustmann, Fabbri and Preston, (2005), The impact of immigration on the UK labour market

Education and Skills Select Committee, (2006), Further education, forth report of the session 2005-06

Eurostat, (1999), Continuing vocational training survey 2

Feinstein, (2002), Quantitative estimates of the social benefits of learning, 1: Crime, Centre for Research on the Wider Benefits of Learning

Feinstein, (2002), Quantitative estimates of the social benefits of learning, 2: Health (depression and obesity), Centre for Research on the Wider Benefits of Learning

Foster, (2005), Realising the potential: A review of the future role of further education colleges, Department for Education and Skills

GHK, (2005), Skills for business network phase 2 evaluation case studies, Research Report 12

Goos and Manning, (2003), Lousy and lovely jobs: the rising polarisation of work in Britain

Government Actuary's Department, (2004), Population projections

Green, Mayhew and Molloy, (2003), Employer perspectives survey,

Greenway and Nelson, Oxford Review of Economic Policy, Volume 16, Number 3, (2000), The assessment: globalisation and labour market adjustments

Higher Education Funding Council England, (2005), Financial forecasts and annual monitoring statements

HM Treasury, (2000), Helping people to save

HM Treasury, (2004), Long-term global economic challenges and opportunities for the UK

HM Treasury, (2002), Developing workforce skills: piloting a new approach

HM Treasury/Sector Skills Development Agency, CE/IER, (2005), Alternative skills scenarios to 2020 for the UK economy: Report to the Leitch Review of Skills

Home Office Command Paper, (2006), A points based system: Making migration work for Britain

Institute for Employment Studies, (2003), Evaluation of Learner support funds

Institute for Employment Studies, (2005), Learner support funds: Second evaluation final report

Institute for Employment Studies, (2006), Employer training pilots: Final evaluation report

Lau and Vase, Office for National Statistics (2002), Accounting growth: capital, skills and output

Lambert , (2003), Lambert review of business-university collaboration, HM Stationary Office,

Leadership and Management Advisory Panel, The, (2006), Leadership and management in the UK: Raising our ambition, Submission to the Leitch Review

Learning Skills Council, (2003), The impact of Adult Information and Advice Services - a summary

Learning Skills Council, (2005), National Employer Skills Survey

Learning Skills Council, (2006), Further education and work-based learning for young people- learner outcomes in 2004/05

Leitch Review of skills, (2005), Skills in the UK: The long-term challenge

Machin, (2003), Higher education, family income and changes in intergenerational mobility, in Dickens, Gregg and Wadsworth (eds), (2003), The labour market under New Labour: The state of working Britain

Machin and Meghir, (2000), Crime and economic incentives, Institute for Fiscal Studies

Manning, CEP Discussion Paper 640, (2004), We can work it out: the impact of technological change on the demand for low-skill workers

McIntosh, CEE, (2004), Further analysis of the returns to academic and vocational qualifications

McIntosh, Dearden, Myck, Vignoles, (2000), The returns to academic, vocational and basic skills in Britain, Skills Task Force research paper 20

OECD, (2006), Education at a Glance

O'Mahoney and de Boer, National Institute for Economic and Social Research, (2002), Britain's relative productivity performance: updates to 1999

Pathways in Adult Learning Survey, (2003)

Price Waterhouse and Coopers, (2005), The market for qualifications in the UK

Scottish Executive, (2003), The life long learning strategy for Scotland

Scottish Executive, (2006), Workforce Plus – An employability framework for Scotland

Sector Skills Development Agency, (2005), Skills for business network: Sectoral productivity differences across the UK, Research Report 13

Sector Skills Development Agency, (2005), Skills for business network: Survey of employers

Sianesi, (2003), Returns to education: A non-technical summary of CEE work and policy discussion, Institute for Fiscal Studies and Centre for the Economics of Education

Sianesi and van Reenan, Institute for Fiscal Studies, (2002), The returns to education: a review of the empirical macroeconomic literature

Small Business Service, (2006), Small and medium-sized enterprise statistics fo the UK, 2005

Small Business Service, (2006), Small Business Service proposals for the 2006 Pre Budget Report

Unionlearn, (2006), Changing lives through learning, a guide to Unionlearn